# Psychometric Testing in Personnel Selection and Appraisal

## Paul Kline

Professor of Psychometrics, University of Exeter

Croner Publications Ltd
Croner House
London Road
Kingston upon Thames
Surrey KT2 6SR

Copyright © 1992 Croner Publications Ltd
First published 1992


Published by
Croner Publications Ltd,
Croner House,
London Road,
Kingston upon Thames,
Surrey KT2 6SR
Tel: 081-547 3333

While every care has been taken
in the writing and editing of this book,
readers should be aware that only Acts of Parliament
and Statutory Instruments have the force of law,
and that only the courts can authoritatively
interpret the law.

British Library Cataloguing in Publication Data
A CIP Catalogue Record for this book
is available from the British Library


ISBN 1 85542 112 9


Typeset by BP Integraphics Ltd., Bath, Avon
Printed by The Bath Press, Bath, Avon

Psychometric Testing in Personnel Selection
and Appraisal

# Contents

# Chapter 1
# Why Use Psychometric Tests?

Before the usefulness of psychometric testing in the work of the personnel manager both for the selection and appraisal of staff and for staff development is put forward, a few terms should be defined and the underlying rationale pointed out.

*Psychometric test.* A psychometric test usually consists of a set of items which have been tried out and found to be satisfactory. The scores obtained by individuals on psychometric tests can be compared with the scores of various other groups, known as norms. The majority of the best known psychological tests would be classified as psychometric tests.

*Psychological test.* Some psychological tests are not psychometric. The Rorschach Test, consisting of a set of inkblots which subjects have to describe, the descriptions being then interpreted by the tester, is not a psychometric test. Similarly laboratory measures of intelligence which make use of reaction times to lights or measure brain waves are not psychometric tests.

*The psychometric model.* Underlying the use of psychometric tests for personnel selection is what might be called the psychometric model of behaviour. It assumes that everything a person does is predictable in terms of abilities, personality, motivation, mood and the particular situation that individual is in. Applied to jobs it means that there is an ideal set of characteristics for each job. The task of psychometric testing is to measure those characteristics as accurately as possible. At present this match of model to job is in its infancy. Indeed I shall argue throughout this book that it is one of the duties of personnel officers and managers to collect together the results of all their testing so that over the years a good data base for fitting people to jobs can be developed and the psychological requirements for jobs can be described. This is what scientific personnel selection demands.

*The advantages of psychometric testing in personnel work.* There are many advantages to using psychometric testing for all types of assessment. Below is a brief list of the most important points in the industrial application of psychometric testing.

Many of these points will be amplified in later chapters of this book.

&#10005; 1   Psychometric tests measure what they claim to measure. The best psychometric tests provide good evidence that they measure what they claim.
This differentiates them from most other methods of appraisal. Interviews,
of course, are probably the most common method of appraisal in the world,
but can be shown usually to add in error to selection procedures. Rating
scales are subject to all kinds of biases, such as the rater's tendency to
use or not use extremes. Appraisal methods such as graphology, or methods
based on the selection of colours are often worthless, although many of
these are widely used in selection procedures.

When the characteristics of good psychological tests are discussed in
the next chapter, the reasons for the failure of these methods will become
evident. A full examination of these problems may be found in Herriot
(1989) or Kline (1992).

&#10005; 2   Norms. The meaning and psychological significance of a test score can
only be interpreted using norms. Almost without exception psychometric
tests are the only measures for which norms are supplied. What constitutes
good norms (for bad ones can be worse than none) will be discussed in
Chapter 3. One of the great advantages of norms is that it is possible
to build up in-house norms, enabling precise and relevant comparisons
to be made.

&#10005; 3   Efficiency. Psychometric tests can be quite short, thus cutting down the
time required for appraisal and enabling more candidates to be tested in
selection procedures. Furthermore the vast majority of psychometric tests
are group tests which means that large numbers can be tested on one
occasion. In big organisations this is a considerable advantage.

4   Computer administration. Many of the best established psychometric tests
can be computer administered. This is particularly valuable where tests
are used in staff development because results are often available immediately
on completion of the test. The printout of results, which can also include
interpretation of the meanings, where required, can then form a basis
for discussion. Full details of this can be found in Chapter 10.

&#10005; 5   Cost efficiency. Throughout this book it will be shown that psychometric
tests, even if imperfect, are the most accurate form of psychological assessment, with some types of test being superior to others. This being the
case there are huge savings to be made by using them, particularly for
jobs where expensive training is involved or where there is a risk of damag-
ing valuable equipment. The most striking example of this is to be seen
in the selection of pilots for high speed low flying jet planes, as used in

2

the recent Gulf war. A selection procedure which eliminated only one pilot who would have failed the training course saves a million pounds. To eliminate one who might have crashed saves much more, quite apart from the human cost of failure and possible death or injury.

6    Fairness. A selection or appraisal procedure with a rational basis, such as that based upon accurate psychometric tests, can be shown and seen to be fair. It hardly needs to be said that a just system is better than a biased or prejudiced procedure. Of course, the use of bad tests is no more fair than any other method, but as shall be seen there are ample tests available for the needs of most jobs and occupations.

The use of psychometric tests can be easily defended where workers object to any of the procedures, say in appraisal. This is in contrast to the use of interviews which often may rest on little more than the intuition of the interviewer and are rarely found convincing by disgruntled and disappointed employees.

These are some of the main advantages of the use of psychometric tests in the work of the personnel manager. There can be little doubt from these arguments that selection and appraisal can be radically improved by such tests. However psychometric tests can be misused and abused, and listed below are the aspects of testing to avoid at all costs in personnel work.

1    The misuse of test scores. Even the best tests are not perfect. To assume that a difference of one point on a test, say of intelligence, means that one individual is more intelligent than the other is quite absurd. The interpretation of differences in scores both for selection and appraisal will be discussed throughout this book as it differs for different tests. It depends also on for what purposes the scores are to be used.

2    Undue reliance on test scores. This point is best exemplified from my own experience of vocational guidance. One counsellor obtained a score on an interest test from his client indicating an interest in musical conducting as a possible job. The counsellor thus advised his client that this would be suitable for him, despite the fact that this person had never played an instrument, to the best of his knowledge had no special ability in music and had not, until that moment, even contemplated such a career. Clearly any sensible test administrator should have discussed the test score first.

3    Failure to use other information. This is really a further aspect of undue reliance on test scores. Psychometric test scores are only one source of information about a person. Such scores should always be interpreted alongside other reliable information, with the stress on *reliable*. Such would include work records and educational achievement.

X    4    Failure to discuss test scores. In some selection situations it may be impossible to discuss test scores with candidates, but where tests have been used in staff development or for internal assessment and promotion, test scores should be discussed. The meaning of all scores and the implications for career and personal development should be discussed. Used in this way testing can be seen as valuable for both employer and employee.

These points, especially the last three, can be summed up under the notion of the humane use of tests. Tests can be regarded as scientific instruments: take the appropriate measurements, and on this basis make clear-cut decisions. As has been argued above, this is inappropriate to personnel work simply because it disregards the human aspect of psychological testing. Misusing tests in the ways suggested above is not only inefficient, it ignores how people feel about themselves, their self esteem and their feelings of worth. To trample on these is simply wrong, quite apart from the fact that it leads to a discontented and thus inefficient work-force.

Thus, although psychometric tests should not be put to mechanical or inhumane use, especially in personnel selection and appraisal, it is possible to use psychometric tests with both high scientific efficiency and humanity. Such a combination is personnel work at its best.

# Chapter 2
# The Characteristics of Good Psychometric Tests

Good psychometric tests should be reliable, valid, discriminating and have properly sampled norms. These terms are discussed below along with an explanation of how tests may be constructed so that they will possess these desirable characteristics. These aspects of occupational testing are important, and it is essential that personnel managers and officers understand these concepts so that they will be able to select from lists and catalogues of tests those that are adequate for their purposes. A list or catalogue of tests, as well as the test manual, should cite evidence of the reliability measurements detailed below.

## The Meaning of Reliability

In psychometrics reliability has two meanings.

1  Internal consistency. A test is said to be reliable if it is internally consistent, which is hardly surprising. To take an analogy with a ruler or tape measure, it would be a pretty poor specimen if a part of it turned out not to measure distance but measured pressure or another variable.
2  Stability over time. A test is also said to be reliable if repeated measures of individuals who have not changed yield the same score. In practical applied testing this is the more important sense of reliability, since it is obvious that if a test gives different scores on different occasions, there is little reason to take any score seriously.

If tests are used for selection or for any purpose which affects the lives of those tested it is essential that the tests are highly reliable over time. Regrettably, as shall be seen in later chapters of this book, many tests which are regularly used in occupational psychology, both in Great Britain and America, fail this simple criterion.

These are the simple definitions and illustrations of the meanings of reliability but these must now be further discussed so that their importance for occupational testing can be understood.

*Information about test reliability.* A question that springs to mind is where is this information on test reliability to be found. Information on reliability, validity and discriminatory power should be given in the manual to the test. If this information is not given in the manual, or if there is no manual, the test should not be used. In discussing reliability, therefore, it makes sense to discuss what should be found in a satisfactory test manual.

*Internal consistency reliability.* A test is not absolutely reliable or completely unreliable. Reliability is measured on a scale, and to understand this measurement and indeed to understand much about psychometric testing a few simple statistical concepts must be explained. One of the most important is correlation, which measures both test reliability and validity.

# Correlation

Suppose there are two sets of scores from 20 applicants for a job, a score on an intelligence test and a score on a test of anxiety. If there were perfect agreement between the sets of scores, ie the person first on intelligence was first on anxiety and the second on intelligence was second on anxiety and so on, we would have a perfect correlation of 1. Similarly if there were complete disagreement and the bottom on one test was top on the other and so on in that way, the correlation would be − 1, indicating complete disagreement between the two sets of scores. Clearly, in actual testing such results are virtually never found. In reality there is usually some degree of agreement or disagreement between sets of scores.

The correlation coefficient measures the degree of agreement between two sets of scores. It runs from 1 to − 1. The higher the correlation the more the two sets of scores overlap. In fact the correlation squared indicates the percentage of agreement between the two sets of scores. Thus a correlation of .8 shows that there was a 64% agreement, a correlation of .2 shows 4%. Negative correlations also show agreement—if the scores on one test are reversed.

*The correlation coefficient.* The correlation coefficient, which is usually computed to show the correlation between sets of scores, is known as the Pearson product-moment correlation (named after the famous statistician). It is usually symbolised as r in test manuals. Sometimes the rank orders of test scores rather than the scores themselves are correlated and the coefficient for this purpose is rho, $\rho$.

The discussion below of how internal consistency reliability is measured will illustrate fully the meaning and significance of reliability as internal consistency.

## Measurement of internal consistency reliability

*Split-half reliability*. In this a test is divided into two parts. For example, the scores on the even items and the scores on the odd items would be given and a correlation computed between them. In a perfectly consistent test this correlation would be 1, which would indicate that each half of the test measured the same variable.

*The alpha coefficient*. In modern psychometric practice the simple split-half reliability is not used, since a test may be divided up in many ways, and one particular split may not provide an accurate index. Coefficient alpha was developed to overcome this problem and is the expected correlation of the set of items with any other comparable set. This is regarded as the best index of internal consistency. In practice, however, it is often highly similar to a simple split-half reliability. Modern test manuals should always set out the alpha coefficient of their tests.

*KR20 coefficient*. This is a simplified form of coefficient alpha, developed by Kuder and Richardson. It is identical to coefficient alpha in the case of dichotomous items, such as personality test items requiring subjects to answer "Yes" or "No". With items of this type it is perfectly in order to set out KR20 reliability coefficients in the test manual.

*The size of the reliability coefficient*. What should the reliability coefficient be if a test is to be considered satisfactory? If a test is to be used with individuals in occupational work the minimum reliability coefficient acceptable is .7. (The basis for this will be discussed later in this chapter.) It should be stressed that .7 is a minimum coefficient. As has been discussed above this means that there is only 49% consistency, which obviously means that 51% of the variance is inconsistent and thus in error. The less reliable a test the more its scores are confounded with error.

How high the reliability should be will depend on the type of test. Tests of intelligence or verbal ability are easy to make highly reliable, a reliability of .7 would not be acceptable for this type of test. Personality tests, on the other hand, are generally less reliable and .7 would be an acceptable figure. What are acceptable reliabilities for the different types of test will be discussed in later chapters of this book.

*The sample from which the reliability coefficient was obtained.* It is important that this sample of subjects was similar to subjects for whom the test is intended. Thus a test which is designed for graduate recruitment should be shown to be reliable among young graduates. Reliability coefficients derived from a sample of schoolchildren or psychiatric outpatients would not be satisfactory.

Furthermore the sample size should be sufficient to reduce the standard error of the correlation. The larger the sample the smaller this error. It should also be large enough to be a reasonably representative sample of the target population. Fifty subjects are the minimum necessary to render the statistical error negligible. In general samples of about 100 subjects are acceptable for establishing the reliability of a test.

# Measurement of test–retest reliability

This is a far more simple matter than the measurement of internal consistency reliability. All that is necessary is to give the test to a sample of subjects representative of the target population and of a sufficient size to reduce statistical error. Again 100 subjects is a satisfactory sample and a minimum figure would be 50 subjects.

The time interval between testing subjects is important. Obviously to test the subjects twice on the same day would produce a spuriously high reliability since many would remember their responses. Similarly a gap of five years might produce spuriously low reliability since some if not all the subjects might have changed in respect of the test variable. Generally a three to six month gap is recommended for the establishment of test-retest reliability.

Subjects may change on the variable. If a test variable being measured is highly volatile, such as a mood or state, then test-retest reliability may not be a sensible criterion. Fortunately in occupational psychology there is little need to measure variables of this type so this is a problem which may be ignored. Tests suitable for occupational use should have high test-retest reliabilities.

Some psychometric tests have parallel forms, which are purportedly identical. These are useful for retesting or where, in a selection process, it is known that the subject has done the same test before. For parallel form tests to be regarded as genuinely identical and thus used interchangeably, the correlation between them should be high. For these purposes the parallel form reliability should be beyond .9. Where this is not the case it is best to use one form and stick to that.

# Factors influencing test reliability

If it is assumed that a consistent set of test items has been written there are various factors which can contribute to test unreliability and these will be briefly noted.

(a) Test length. Ten items is the minimum length for a reliable test. After that, the more items a test has the more reliable it becomes, unless it becomes so long that fatigue and boredom set in.

(b) Objective marking. The scoring should be objective, requiring no judgement from the scorers. This is the major problem with the interview as a method of assessment.

(c) Clear test instructions. If the instructions for subjects taking the test are not clear, for example of how to record the correct answer, this leads to unreliability.

(d) Testing conditions. If testing conditions are poor, for example too cramped, too warm, or an imperfect keyboard for a computer test, this adds to error and thus contributes to low reliability.

(e) Personal problems. Obviously on any given day some subjects will be upset, ill, tired, depressed, or feeling exceptionally well. All these affect the reliability of the test.

The importance of high reliability for the tests used in occupational psychology cannot be stressed too much, as the higher the reliability the more accurate the score, thus leading to more effective personnel procedures.

For the reasons discussed above, there can be error in any one score which is obtained from a subject. If this subject was tested on many occasions and an average or mean of the scores was taken this score would be more accurate. Repeated testing is, of course, generally impossible. However it is possible to estimate how accurate a score is by calculating the *standard error* of a score. If a subject were tested many times, 68% of scores would fall between the obtained score and one standard error of the score, while 95% of all scores would fall between two standard errors. An example will clarify the point.

If a subject scores 100 on a test and the standard error is 1 then 95% of that subject's scores would fall between 102 and 98. Thus this score of 100 is definitely superior to a score of 90 and inferior to a score of 105, but could not be considered different to a score of 99 or 101. The standard error of a score is highly important in making personnel decisions, and is intimately related to the reliability of the test. The higher the reliability the lower this standard error. It is for this reason that .7 is the criterion for an acceptable test (although this is lower than desirable).

## Validity of tests

A test, as has been stated, is said to be valid if it measures what it purports to measure. Almost certainly, except in special cases, high reliability is a necessary but not the only condition for validity. Validity is a term with many somewhat different meanings and these must now be discussed.

*Face validity.* Face validity refers to the appearance of a test. If a test looks valid it has face validity. Unfortunately, in many kinds of test which are frequently used in personnel work, face validity bears no relation to actual validity. Indeed if items are too transparent it can lead to "faking good" especially where the tests are used for selection.

Face validity is important in applied psychology to maintain the cooperation and attention of subjects. If the test appears to be nonsense and irrelevant to their case, subjects will not take it seriously and scores will be distorted. Thus face valid as well as genuinely valid tests are desirable. How faking can be reduced or minimised by proper selection of tests will be discussed in the chapters devoted to those tests where such problems are likely to arise.

*Concurrent validity.* The concurrent validity of a test is measured by its correlation with other similar tests. Since the correlation of a test is limited by its reliability which, as has been discussed, is always less than 1, concurrent validity can only rarely be expected to be greater than .9. In practice a concurrent validity coefficient of .65 would be an acceptable minimum.

The great difficulty with concurrent validity concerns the criterion test. In most areas of psychological testing there is no benchmark test of fully accepted validity. Indeed only in the field of intelligence and extraversion and neuroticism are such benchmark tests available. Therefore correlations with similar, but imperfect tests, could not be expected to be high. Usually concurrent validity indices are in the order of .4 to .5. Such coefficients can be regarded as supporting rather than definitive evidence of validity.

There is a further problem. If there is a benchmark test why should another test be required? The only reason for a new test where a benchmark test exists is extra convenience, for example a group test rather than an individual test or a test which takes 10 minutes rather than an hour. This last is a vital consideration

10

in personnel work where time is money and brief testing is always preferable provided that it is not at the expense of validity.

It should be made clear that concurrent validity is useful but often it is suggestive rather than definitive.

*Predictive validity.* A test is said to have predictive validity if it can predict some criterion score. For example, an intelligence test which could predict academic performance several years later would be considered to have predictive validity. Its validity would be indexed by the correlation between the test score and some measure of academic achievement.

Predictive validity is firm evidence that a test measures what it claims to measure, and is particularly relevant in occupational selection. Thus any test which could predict success at a particular job could be said to be a valid test for selection for that position. This example makes the more general point that test validity is validity for some task: in this case selection for this particular job.

A problem with predictive validity is that often there is no clear criterion to be predicted making the demonstration of predictive validity impossible. Thus it is by no means apparent what criteria might be set up for establishing the predictive validity of a test of extraversion or openness to experience, which are variables thought to be important in the measurement of personality.

Again, as was the case with concurrent validity, the size of the correlation in predictive validity studies is usually moderate and predictive validity is somewhat subjective. In studies of validity, unlike reliability, there is no unequivocal validity coefficient.

*Incremental validity.* If a large number of tests is given in a selection procedure it may well be the case that one particular test correlates rather low with the criterion score but is completely uncorrelated with the other tests in the selection battery. In this instance this test is said to have incremental validity. Overall the use of such a test would improve the prediction from the battery of tests, because, as the absence of correlation shows, it is measuring something different from the other tests. However, in practice it is rare for a test to correlate with the criterion but not the other tests. Nevertheless in occupational selection incremental validity can be important.

*Construct validity.* The best evidence for the validity of a test is often its construct validity. To demonstrate the construct validity of a test hypotheses are set up concerning the results to be expected from the test if it were valid. These hypotheses are then investigated and if the majority are supported the test is said to possess construct validity. All these experiments supporting the construct validity of a test should be reported in the test manual. The following example of mechanical ability tests will clarify the issue and, as will be seen, construct validity embraces all the other types which have been described.

This test of mechanical ability should correlate with other tests of mechanical ability, but not with tests of personality or interest, except perhaps mechanical interest. Scores on this test should predict ability in engineering which will be measured by admission to engineering courses, passes in engineering examinations and performance in engineering. Engineers should score more highly than controls on this test. If all these hypotheses are supported it is clear that the construct validity of the test as measuring mechanical ability is confirmed for no other variable would yield such results.

These are the main meanings of validity. All test manuals should cite evidence for all or some of these types of validity, in which some degree of judgement is involved. If no evidence other than face validity for the validity of a test is presented in the manual it should not be used, especially in occupational psychology where decisions based on test results are so vital to all subjects and for the organisation selecting the candidates.

# Discriminatory power

In selection and in most other personnel work, a test which fails to discriminate among subjects, that is on which all subjects received the same score, would be useless (and almost certainly invalid) unless the purpose of the test was to ensure that subjects scored above a certain threshold score. In general, however, the more discriminating a test the better it is. Discriminatory power is reflected in the spread of scores around the mean score (the variance) and in the shape of the distribution.

The discriminatory power of a test is measured by the statistic delta. The most discriminating test possible has a delta of one. This occurs when there is a horizontal distribution of scores, that is an equal number of the sample scores each possible score on the test. This obviously maximises the spread of scores or variance, but such a distribution is extremely rare in practice. A test with a normal distribution of scores, where the frequency of individuals scoring each possible score follows the bell shaped Gaussian curve, discriminates well and has a delta of .93. In general a test should have a delta of beyond .9, a criterion which in fact the majority of psychometric tests meet.

In this chapter the meanings of reliability, validity and discriminatory power have been discussed and their importance and significance for occupational testing have been pointed out. These are the characteristics of any good psychological test or of any kind of scientific measure. In Chapter 3 a further important aspect of good psychometric tests—test norms—will be examined.

# Chapter 3
# Test Norms

The fourth characteristic of good psychometric tests is to be well standardised and possess good norms, which present problems and demands discussed below.

## Norms

Norms are sets of scores from designated groups. Their importance lies in the fact that comparison with norms gives psychological meaning to a subject's score. Thus norms are critical for psychological tests since these have no meaningful zero. The scale or metric of any test is to some extent arbitrary for this reason. However, as soon as a score can be compared with norms this lack of meaning disappears provided that the normative groups have been properly constituted.

## Standardisation

Standardisation refers to this setting up of the normative groups and the problems and difficulties involved in this must be scrutinised since it is obvious that if the norms are bad, test interpretation will be weakened if not absolutely misleading.

Good norms and standardisation are particularly important in all forms of personnel appraisal and selection. For example, if it is known that a particular post demands a high degree of spatial ability, then subjects might be required who score in the top 5% on this variable. If the norms for this test are based on a small and unrepresentative sample of the population, a score which appears to meet this criterion may, in fact, not do so, and selection will be inefficient.

# Sampling in Standardisation

Sampling is the critical feature of setting up good norms. As was the case with reliability, validity and discriminatory power, full details of the normative sample or samples should be given in the test manual. If they are not, it would be risky to put much reliance in the norms. Suffice it to say that many otherwise good tests fall down at the normative stage usually because the cost of establishing good norms is considerable. However, as shall be seen, for the personnel worker all may not be lost, even if the norms are imperfect.

There are two variables involved in sampling and these will be discussed separately: the size of the sample and its representativeness.

*Sample size.* All descriptive statistics such as the mean or average and the standard deviation (which measures the spread of the scores, the variance) possess standard errors indicating what these figures might be on further testing. All these standard errors decrease as the sample size increases. With samples of 500 or more these standard errors are negligible. Thus, on this criterion, 500 is an adequate normative sample. However a statistically accurate but unrepresentative sample is not useful.

A normative sample must be representative, and the size of sample needed to reflect adequately its population depends upon the size of the population and its homogeneity. For example there are about 5000 university professors in Great Britain and a sample of 500 could be representative of this relatively homogeneous group. However such a sized sample would not reflect the diversity of the general population.

The question therefore arises as to how a normative sample can be judged to be satisfactory given that there is no absolute number which guarantees its quality.

*Representative samples.* From the discussion of the paragraphs above it is clear that to have a representative sample there is more involved than size. How is the diversity of a population to be represented? All this turns on sampling methods and these must now be briefly discussed. Actually sampling is a complex process and here I shall simply summarise the necessities of a good sample. A full discussion may be found in Kline (1992).

There are two methods of obtaining satisfactory normative samples, by random and by stratified sampling.

1   Random sampling. A sample may be said to be random if there is an equal chance that any member of the population can be a member of the sample. With random sampling a large sample can be truly representative. If the important categories of a population from whom a sample is required are unknown random sampling is the best method. However,

this description requires two further points to be expanded. What constitutes a large sample and how is random sampling actually to be carried out?

(a) Defining the population. If a sample is to be genuinely random it is necessary to define the population. I shall take as an example the adult population of Great Britain. Theoretically this is simple to define but for the purposes of sampling an operational definition is required. Ideally a list of adults would provide a sampling base. However such a list is almost impossible to obtain. Censuses are rapidly out of date; voting lists are usually incomplete, especially so since the poll tax; telephone directories are class biased as are lists of customers for various consumer goods. A genuinely random sample of adults is difficult to achieve.

Of course in personnel work general population norms may be less useful than norms for specialised groups. If the task is to select electrical engineers norms for these would be most desirable. However here again it is hard to draw random samples of electrical engineers although it is possible that their professional body contains a relatively complete list.

In practice norms for occupational groups consist often of what the test constructors were able to obtain. Electrical engineers from three companies or even from one company would not be unusual. These are better than nothing but have clearly to be used with caution.

(b) If a list can be obtained each subject is given a number and a set of random numbers, generated by computer, yields the sample. Another method is to randomise the list and select every jth individual, j being fixed by the proportion of the population in the sample. Unfortunately to be representative this needs to be large, thus leading to large samples which are expensive to test and time consuming and for this reason stratified sampling is often used.

2   Stratified sampling. Cattell, who is one of the leading test constructors, has always argued that a stratified sample is more effective than a random sample of the same size and is therefore to be preferred. This is the approach to test standardisation which Cattell and colleagues use (eg Cattell et al, 1970). Their argument is certainly true given that the stratification is correct.

Stratified sampling involves dividing a heterogeneous population into a number of homogeneous groups. These are then sampled and the combination of these samples provides a good cross-section of the original population. Since homogeneous populations require smaller samples to be representative than do heterogeneous populations it follows that stratified samples must be more adequate size for size than random samples, as has been argued.

Which variables are used to stratify a population is a critical issue. If too many variables are chosen, then the sample will be enormous. If the wrong variables are used the sample will not be representative. Fortunately there are two simple rules in stratifying a sample. The stratifying variables must be correlated with the test for which norms are being established and the number of variables should be minimised: four variables are usually sufficient.

An example is stratified sampling from the American general population norms for the 16PF Test (Cattell et al, 1970), a personality test. The US was divided into 8 population areas and 8 population densities. The population was divided into 5 age groups and 7 income groups. Then the percentages in the population of each of these groups was reflected as accurately as possible in a sample size of 1000 women.

However when the numbers in some of these stratified categories are examined it is found that they are clearly far too small to be representative: 30 in the mountain area and 239 in the two categories of large cities with populations greater than two million.

Indeed, if a stratified sample were drawn based upon two sexes, five social classes and five age groups, this produces 50 categories. Furthermore if 300 subjects was regarded as the minimum sample for each category, then over 15,000 subjects would be included in the sample. To test so many is costly and time consuming and simply beyond the resources of most test constructors.

# Special group norms

For such reasons many test constructors prefer to use specific group norms because these can be smaller. All the same principles of random and of stratified sampling apply to setting up norms for special groups but because they are more homogeneous samples can be representative and relatively small. To use the example of engineers again, these could be stratified by type of employer, self-employed, consultant, working in large firms, medium and small firms. If the numbers in these groups reflected the numbers in the population a reasonably representative sample of about 500 could be drawn up.

For personnel selection well stratified occupational norms, where it is clear that the normative groups are representative and large enough to reduce standard error (in real rather than academic life 100 subjects might be sufficient), are the most valuable.

## House norms

Sometimes even more useful than specific group norms are house norms. These consist of the scores of workers in various jobs in the organisation where the test is being used.

Sometimes a new test is developed which has good evidence for its validity and reliability but which has no norms other than a few students or a small sample of the general population. Such a test might be introduced into a selection system in a large organisation, and used only after a few years when house norms had been built up. For example it might be found that successful graduate trainees had certain scores on the test. Such house norms would be highly useful in selection, probably more valuable than specific or general group norms. Such house norms are only suited to large organisations dealing with several hundreds of employees over a few years.

From this discussion it is clear that to establish adequate norms requires considerable resources. The problems involved are largely practical. It is also the case that most psychometric tests do not meet the standards of standardisation which I have discussed. In the real world this is hardly surprising. Nevertheless the more the norms are based on groups which do not meet these criteria the more cautiously should they be used in interpreting the scores.

# Types of Norm

The scores of normative groups can be expressed in a number of ways. The advantages and disadvantages of the different types of norms will now be examined.

## Percentiles

A percentile is the score below which a given percentage of the normative group fall. Thus the 80th percentile is the score below which 80% of the group fall.

Percentiles are readily understood by people who know nothing about testing and are thus useful in explaining and discussing results. However they have certain disadvantages which render their use dubious.

1   Percentiles are not suited to most types of statistical analysis.
2   Converting raw scores to percentiles exaggerates small differences around the mean and minimises relatively large differences at the tails of the distribution.

For these reasons percentiles are not regarded as a useful form of score other than for simple explanatory purposes.

## Standard scores

Standard scores are the most useful type of norm and those most suited to personnel selection and appraisal will be described. The great advantage of all types of standard score is that within each type the same score has the same significance. This allows meaningful comparison of scores on different tests.

*Z scores*. These are the most basic form of standard score with means of 0 and ranges of approximately $+3$ to $-3$. These are not recommended because subjects find it difficult to realise that a score of 1 is relatively good and a score of 2 excellent. However z scores can easily be transformed into other more user-friendly scores of which the most common are scores with a mean of 50 and a standard deviation of 10. The standard deviation measures the scatter of scores around the mean. Generally the range is six times the standard deviation. Thus these standard scores would tend to run from 20 to 80. This is certainly the most useful form of standard score.

*Normalised standard scores*. Z scores can be transformed and normalised. This means that the resulting normative scores have a normal, bell shaped distribution. There are four commonly used norms of this type.

1   T scores. These are normally distributed standard scores with a mean of 50 and a standard deviation of 10. Because they are normally distributed it is possible to convert these scores to percentiles, for ease of explanation.
2   Stanines. Here the normal distribution is broken down into a 9-point scale, with a mean of 5 and a standard deviation of 2.
3   Stens. In this scale the normal distribution is broken into a 10-point scale, with a mean of 5.5 and a standard deviation of 1.5.
4   Scales with a mean of 100 and a standard deviation of 15. These are used for intelligence tests and give rise to the notion of the average IQ as 100.

Normalised scores should only be used where, as in the case of intelligence tests, there is good reason to think that the scores should be normally distributed. Where this is not the case a standard score such as the scale with a mean of 50 and a standard deviation of 10 is probably the best.

# Ipsative scores

One should be aware of the nature of ipsative scores, since these are often misused in personnel psychology. Ipsative scores are found where there are forced choices between items and where each choice is scored. For example in some tests of interests subjects have to rank in order a number of activities.

In tests of this kind norms are impossible because an individual's scores represent that person's relative strength of interests. For example a light drinker might rank his favourite drinks as whisky, gin and vodka. This ranking would mean something quite different from the same rankings from an alcoholic. Norms derived from rankings, when all the meanings were different, would not be sensible.

It should be pointed out that ipsative scores are negatively correlated by virtue of their scoring system and thus quite unsuited to factor analysis which makes it difficult to identify the meaning of the scores. In addition since norms are not meaningful it follows that ipsative tests are only suited to those testing contexts where the scores are discussed with the subjects, as in vocational guidance and counselling and in career development. However it is to be noted that the quantification offered by these tests is relatively unimportant. The results from ipsative tests are valuable only as bases for discussion.

# Chapter 4
# Selecting the Right Tests

In Chapters 2 and 3 the characteristics of good psychological tests were described and discussed. Clearly these are important in selecting the right test for any particular purpose. However the mere fact that a test is reliable and valid does not mean that it is suitable. How are tests matched to jobs? How does the test user choose between equally valid tests of the same variable? How does the tester know what tests are available? All these and similar questions will be addressed in this chapter.

## Lists of psychometric tests

*The Mental Measurement Yearbooks.* Buros (eg 1972) produced a series of Mental Measurement Yearbooks, every five years. These have continued since his death and each contains as full a list as possible of tests published in Great Britain and America. These tests are described and in many cases evaluated by experts in the field. These volumes constitute an excellent source of information about tests. However these are huge volumes and as the majority of tests reviewed there are not of high quality and many are of no relevance to occupational psychology, many occupational testers would regard the Yearbooks as simply too large for their purposes. Nevertheless, they constitute the best reference source for tests. It must be stressed, however, that being in Buros is no guarantee of the quality or suitability of a test for any purpose. One of the most useful bits of information about each test which is to be found in Buros is its publisher and distributors.

*Tests in print.* Buros also produces from time to time a summary of these Mental Measurement Yearbooks—Tests in Print. Although huge volumes, these list the tests more succinctly and refer readers to evaluations in the Mental Measurement Yearbooks, although some evaluations are reprinted. In general I have found that these Tests in Print are not useful on their own but they do help finding the relevant volume of the Yearbooks.

For personnel testers who are using a variety of tests both for selection and appraisal, the latest edition of the Mental Measurement Yearbooks is an invaluable resource.

*Test catalogues.* In Great Britain a small number of publishers and test agencies supply psychological tests and their catalogues obviously contain useful lists of tests categorised by type and purpose. These are all commercial operations and their claims cannot be taken on trust. This is not to say that they are false and, indeed, these distributors and publishers have attempted to supply the best tests of their type. Nevertheless it is necessary to evaluate all the tests in the light of the psychometric criteria of reliability, validity, and standardisation, as has been discussed.

# Distributors

All distributors of tests in this country cannot be listed but three stand out as dealing with a range of the best tests available.

*Oxford Psychologists Press.* This test distributor offers a range of tests which is designed for occupational psychologists and many of the tests which they offer would be agreed by almost all psychometrists as being among the best of their kind. Some, however, I would judge to be weak, although, obviously, the directors of this press who are all psychologists do not agree. They have tests in the fields of: personality; interpersonal and organisational variables; occupational stress; career planning and development; ability, aptitude and cognitive style, self-esteem and adjustment.

*The Psychological Corporation.* This sells some of the best known psychological tests although many of them are more suited to educational, clinical and medical psychology than to occupational work. However, the corporation is a major test importer and publisher and their list may widen to include tests more likely to be useful to the occupational psychologist and tester. Their catalogue is certainly worthy of scrutiny.

*NFER-Nelson.* The letters NFER stood originally for National Foundation for Educational Research and the origins of this test distributor and publisher were in this area. However, over the years they have widened their interests and they deal with a large number of tests highly useful in occupational work, including some of the best known personality inventories. Recently NFER–Nelson have formed a special division for occupational testing known as ASE and it is this section which should be contacted concerning test materials.

These are the three largest publishers and distributors of tests in Great Britain, but there are many others some of whose products would be useful for occupational psychology. These may be found in the *Mental Measurement Yearbooks* which have already been described.

*American test publishers.* In America psychology as a university subject and occupational psychology as a career is considerably more developed than in Great Britain. As a consequence of this, the vast majority of psychometric tests are American. As a result many of the best tests are also American. This can mean that they are hard to obtain in Great Britain if there is no British importer.

Some American test publishers respond remarkably quickly to requests for tests but with others there are difficulties. Nevertheless it is worth noting some of the American test publishers and distributors whose lists may prove useful.

IPAT, based in Champaign, Illinois, distributes mainly tests developed by Cattell and colleagues. These include some of the finest tests of ability, personality and motivation ever produced even though some of them may now be at the end of their development. IPAT sends tests to England virtually by return and, in some cases, has beaten their British distributor for speed of delivery.

Other important American test distributors and publishers who handle the type of tests which are likely to be useful for occupational and personnel testing are: Consulting Psychologists Press; The Psychological Corporation; Science Research Associates; Educational Testing Service; Sheridan Psychological Services and Western Psychological Services.

All these companies deal with excellent occupational tests. However, some of their tests will have British distributors and it is usually more simple to obtain the tests from these. However the catalogues of these American publishers are useful as valuable lists of tests.

Educational Testing Service is not only a publisher of psychometric tests, they research and develop their own instruments and they have been responsible for some of the major advances in psychometric theory. Sheridan is the publisher of Guilford's tests and these are among the best of their kind.

# Books

A number of books on psychometrics or psychological testing contain descriptions and evaluations of psychological tests. The more recent these are the better, for obvious reasons, but the lists in these books cannot be as up-to-date as is desirable, although, in fact, many of the best tests have a long history of development. The two best known American psychometric texts are those of Cronbach (1984) and Anastasi (1976). There are no recent British comprehensive accounts of psychological testing other than that of the present author: *A Handbook of Psychological Testing* (Kline, 1992). All these three texts include useful descriptions and discussions of tests suitable for occupational selection and appraisal.

# Articles

Various psychological journals contain studies of the validity of tests and descriptions of new tests which have been developed. These latter may seem highly interesting but they should not be used until a manual has been produced which gives details of reliability, validity and norms, as set out in Chapter 3.

As regards studies of the validity of tests it is only recommended that these articles are read by those who feel confident that they can evaluate psychometric research. Many such papers claim that tests are or are not valid and yet are flawed in some aspect of design and analysis which infirms the results. Typical journals where papers are to be found are: *Occupational Psychology*, *Personality and Individual Differences* and *Applied Psychological Measurement*. In brief these journals are useful but only for experts.

Such are the sources of information about tests. From these it is possible to get some idea as to what tests might be suitable for the necessary tasks. However from these catalogues and evaluative descriptions no more than a long-list of tests can be drawn. From such a list the final selection still has to be made. Before the criteria for this final selection are discussed, a little needs to be said about buying psychological tests.

# Purchase of Tests

To purchase psychological tests from reputable publishers and distributors certain qualifications are deemed necessary. In Great Britain these organisations have agreed with the British Psychological Society what qualifications are required for each test. These vary according to the type of test, and to a minor extent with test publishers. However, the rules used by ASE (discussed above) are typical and are set out below.

1   Psychologists with a recognised Masters degree in occupational, educational or clinical psychology are allowed access to all types of tests. Effectively this means that in any organisation which wants to use a wide variety of tests one individual should have a Masters degree in occupational

24

psychology. Such a person can supervise the administration and interpretation of tests by those less qualified.

2   Psychologists without a professional qualification (usually a first degree in psychology) must negotiate which tests can be purchased and this depends upon the particular training and experience which an individual has had. Such a person can usually administer the tests likely to be valuable in occupational selection and appraisal.

3   For non-psychologists ASE and most other test distributors and publishers run special, brief (4 or 5 days) training courses which allow people to buy ability tests and further courses to use specific personality tests. Thus with approximately 14 days' training it is possible to gain access to tests which would be suitable for many selection purposes. This is certainly the route chosen by many engaged in personnel selection.

It must be said, however, that in my view occupational testing done by those with only brief training is unlikely to be as effective as that done by a good occupational psychologist.

*Final selection of tests.* As has been argued, from books, catalogues and articles a long-list of possible tests could be drawn up. How the final selection is to be made must now be discussed.

1   Using the test manual. In the previous chapter the following qualities of good tests were carefully examined.

   (a) Reliability. Any test to be used must have a reliability not lower than .7.

   (b) Validity. Any test to be used must have clear evidence for validity. Ideally this evidence should relate to its ability to discriminate among occupational groups or to correlate with success at the relevant jobs.

   (c) Norms. The test norms should be large and representative. Ideally the relevant occupational norms should be there.

   Tests that pass these three criteria are suitable for occupational work.

2   Two further criteria may be invoked if it is necessary to select from tests which have attained the standards discussed above.

   (a) Test length. All other things equal, it is sensible to use the shortest test possible. However, as was mentioned in the previous chapter, since short tests are not as reliable as long tests, all other things are not usually equal.

   (b) Level of difficulty. In the case of ability tests, it is important to choose a test with the correct level of difficulty for the individuals who are to be tested. This is always made clear in the test manual.

It is clear that it is relatively simple from a perusal of test catalogues, books, articles and test manuals to come up with a number of reliable valid and well-standardised tests. However all this begs perhaps the most important aspect of test selection—which variables should be tested.

# Choosing the Right Variables

Intelligence, extroversion, anxiety, interest in outdoor activities, rage: all these are variables. Once it has been decided that extroversion and, say, persistence, are essential for a particular job, then these are the variables to test and all that has been discussed so far in this chapter comes into play in selecting the best tests. There are various approaches to the selection of variables and these are set out below.

It is possible to select the most important ability, personality and motivational variables, as described in psychometric studies of those areas. These are set out in *A Handbook of Psychological Testing*:

*Ability.* Fluid and crystallised intelligence; retrieval ability (fluency in words is an example); visualising ability (important in engineering and architecture); cognitive speed. The best tests of these variables are discussed in Chapter 6.

*Personality.* Extroversion; anxiety or neuroticism; conventionality; conservatism; tough-mindedness. The best tests of these variables are described in Chapter 7.

*Motivation.* Here there is less agreement about the important variables but the best tests to use for measuring interest and motivation are discussed in Chapter 8.

These variables have been shown in psychometric studies to be the most important in their field. This means that these account for much of the variability in personality and ability.

The advantage of using these variables is that because they are the largest in variance they are bound to correlate, to some extent, with performance in virtually all jobs and to discriminate between occupations, thus making them useful for selection and appraisal.

However, the disadvantage is that these correlations and discriminations are likely to be small. An example will clarify the point. Suppose it were necessary to select a copywriter for the manuals and descriptions of engineering products or computers. For this post verbal ability is essential together with knowledge of computing. Neither of these variables is part of the test battery based upon the most important variables. Hence it would not be as effective as one which included these tests.

This raises the original question of what are the best tests for different occupations.

# Task and job analysis

In task and job analyses occupations and jobs are studied to discover exactly what qualities are required to carry them out. There are various methods for these analyses which must be briefly described. Jewell and Siegall (1990) and Kline (1992) contain more detailed accounts of these procedures. In fact, interviews, observations and questionnaires can be used.

*Interviews*. Jewell and Siegall (1990) argue that the best approach to discovering what is involved in a job is to ask those who do it. The problem here is that such interviewing is highly skilled and inexperienced interviewers are likely to produce unreliable results.

*Observations*: task analysis and description. In this approach a minutely detailed description of what is entailed in a job is set out. When this is done the characteristics or traits required become obvious. However, this again is a highly skilled and specialised task. It is necessary to observe the job being done and to locate it in respect of the purpose of the whole organisation.

This should be contrasted with a general job description, based simply upon common sense and intuition, which can be quite misleading. For example, it is often assumed that accountants need mathematical skills. Job analysis reveals, however, that the mathematics used is not difficult and no high level ability in mathematics is actually required. Similarly general job descriptions may fail to identify crisis points in procedures which detailed job analyses could reveal. Thus in the M1 plane crash there were no emergency procedures requiring the cabin crew to report to the flight deck when they saw that an engine was on fire. It was assumed, falsely, that the pilots could see their engines.

Thus detailed task analyses and descriptions based on observations can reveal what is required to carry out a job. However, it should be noted that these requirements are still hypotheses. They could be wrong although they are less likely to be so than those derived from general job descriptions. Furthermore such work is costly and time consuming. For this reason questionnaires are often preferred.

*Questionnaires*. A number of questionnaires have been developed to assess the demands of different jobs. I shall briefly describe one of the best of these—*The Position Analysis Questionnaire, PAQ*. (McCormick et al, 1972). This consists of 194 items relating to five aspects of a job: work output, mental processes, infor-

·mation input, relationships with other people and a general category of other characteristics.

Studies of the validity of this PAQ indicate that 12 variables are measured which allow a job to be assessed. These include physical activity, operating a machine, performing routine activities and decision-making, for example. However, as Jewell and Siegall (1990) point out, not all jobs can be assessed by the PAQ and furthermore these 12 categories offer little more than a common sense description.

It is clear that job assessment is best done by task analysis but this is costly and thus many jobs have not been so described. Questionnaires are better than interviews because they are easier to administer and more reliable, although they cannot provide the detailed insights of task analysis. General descriptions are not recommended even though, in some cases, they may be adequate.

However, in Great Britain, task analyses and descriptions are not readily available. Indeed questionnaire descriptions are not well known. Thus these are not as useful for choosing tests as they ought to be. Fortunately one other approach is possible.

*Correlations with job success and discriminations among occupational groups.* Some of the tests most widely used in occupational psychology contain in their manuals two sets of information both of which are useful in test selection.

(a) Correlations with job success. Some test manuals will show correlations with success at various jobs. Thus the procedure is to find the relevant job or the one which is most similar to it and select the scales from the test which correlate most highly with success at it. In other words tests are selected if they correlate significantly with success at the relevant jobs. Sometimes beta weights between success at the job and the test scales are given. These beta weights indicate how important a test is in predicting success. Here the scales with the highest beta weights are selected.

(b) Occupational discriminations. In test manuals the scales which discriminate one occupational group from another can be found. For example in the manual to the 16PF test the profiles on the 16 scales of different occupational groups are set out. For the relevant occupation select those scales on which the job occupants are at the extreme.

Thus, selecting variables this way ensures that the variables used either correlate with success or discriminate the group from comparable groups.

Ideally for each job the characteristics necessary for success, as found by task analysis or questionnaire study, the correlations of success with psychological variables and the variables which discriminated holders of that job from others, would be set out. Such an encyclopaedia of job specifications would put the choice of test variables onto a rational basis. However, no such encyclopaedia exists although as records are stored on computer in different organisations the compilation of such a text should be possible, in the future, and it should be easily accessed by computer.

Without this it is necessary to make do with the results to be found in the manuals of the leading tests (which will be described in later chapters of this book) and to use common sense about the nature of the job.

In practice it would seem best to select the variables from the most important factors which seem relevant, plus any others which can discriminate the group or predict success at the job, together with any which a common sense job description might suggest.

# Chapter 5
# Different Types of Psychological Test

In Chapter 4 reference was made, in selecting the appropriate tests for a particular purpose, to different types of tests: ability tests, personality tests and tests of interest and motivation. In this chapter these different categories of tests will be described and defined and the basis of these distinctions will be scrutinised. This will make it easier to understand the use of the various types of tests in personnel selection and appraisal, matters to be discussed in subsequent chapters of this book.

## Ability tests

Ability tests, as the name suggests, attempt to measure human abilities. This definition, however, is worthless, unless human abilities are defined, or, at least, described. Abilities may be defined as the capacity to solve problems of various kinds in different areas of human endeavour. Intelligence may be thought of, in this approach to the conceptualisation of human ability, as a general reasoning ability applicable to a wide range of problems, while mathematical ability, on the other hand, obviously refers to mathematical problem solving and is thus more narrow.

A difficulty with this concept of human abilities arises from the fact that their number might be infinite. Does every human activity demand a separate ability? Accounting, bookkeeping, store-checking, filing, computing, programming . . . there is literally no end.

Fortunately this problem has been solved by the application of factor analysis, a statistical method which has been specially developed in psychometrics and which was originally devised to solve this precise problem—the number and nature of human abilities.

*Factor analysis.* It is necessary to break off from the delineation of human abilities and their tests to describe factor analysis because it has been used throughout psychometrics to establish the most important variables for tests and in actual test construction.

Factor analysis is computationally complex so I shall make no attempt to describe its algebra. Clear accounts of this may be found in Child (1991) or Kline (1991). The essence of the method can, however, be simply explained. Suppose that a large number of tests of different abilities had been administered to a large sample of workers in the civil service. Analysis would show that all these scores were positively correlated. Ability in one sphere was related to ability in another. The question then arises as to whether these correlations might be explained by a lesser number of factors. Thus three factors might be supposed to account for the correlations: intelligence, verbal ability, and mathematical ability. Intelligence would explain the fact that all the scores were correlated, verbal ability that the verbal tests were more highly correlated with each other than with other tests and vice versa for mathematical ability. Factor analysis is simply a mathematical procedure, which explains the correlations mathematically with a smaller number of factors. A factor is an addition of a set of scores.

When factors emerge from the factor analysis all that is known is that this set of factors will explain the correlations. What each factor is has to be worked out from the factor loadings which are the correlations of each test with the factor. Thus a factor might emerge which loaded on the following tests: intelligence, verbal comprehension, French, Spanish, vocabulary and rhyming. It is an easy inference that this is verbal ability. Similarly a factor which loaded on mathematics, physics, accounting, chemistry and computing might be identified as mathematical ability. Thus essentially factor analysis is a method of discovering basic underlying dimensions or factors which account mathematically for the correlations between tests.

Over the years since the turn of the century all fields of testing have been subjected to factor analysis to discover the most important dimensions in the field. In this way different kinds of tests can be identified. Thus correlations among ability tests form a set of factors which constitute the most important ability variables. These tests do not correlate to any important extent with personality variables which themselves may be accounted for by a small number of factors. Thus the most important variables or dimensions in the various fields of psychology have been identified by factor analysis and it is these which the various categories of tests should measure.

From this it can be seen that the different categories of test have been identified by factor analysis.

Thus ability tests are tests concerned with problem solving in the different

areas of human behaviour. Factor analysis has revealed which are the most important dimensions of ability and these and their tests will be discussed in the next
chapter.

Here it will be sufficient briefly to list some of the most important dimensions
of ability and to say something about the general characteristics of ability tests.

(a) Intelligence tests. Intelligence tests measure general reasoning ability as
it is applied in the solution of problems of every kind. The intelligence
factor used to be referred to as g or general ability but modern work
has divided this into two correlated factors which will be discussed in
the next chapter: fluid intelligence, which is basic reasoning ability innate
and not strongly influenced by environmental experience, and crystallised
intelligence which is the social emanation of fluid ability. This differs from
culture to culture and the fluid ability of individuals is invested in the
skills which that culture most prizes. Thus in the West crystallised intelligence would be apparent in performance in technological subjects and
academic pursuits. Clearly in non-industrial societies it would be evidenced
in other skills. Intelligence is implicated in almost all skilled occupations.

(b) Major ability tests. Factor analysis has also identified a small number of
large group factors which account for the variance in a large number of
ability tests. These include: verbal, mathematical and spatial ability. Verbal
ability is important for journalists and politicians, spatial ability for architects
and engineers, for example.

(c) Specific ability tests. In addition to this various abilities have been identified
which are relatively specific but may be important for certain kinds of
jobs. The best example of this is musical ability although its value in selection
is limited since for most musical positions actual attainment is far more
important than a test.

It should be noted that specific abilities should be identified empirically,
through factor analysis. It is not possible to infer abilities from the nature
of a job. Thus computer programming ability is specialised but it is com-
prised of a number of characteristics and its relative rarity is accounted
for by the fact that these must occur together, at a reasonably high level,
in the same individual.

The notion of ability at computer programming leads neatly to the second
category of psychological tests.

# Aptitude tests

The term aptitude refers to two distinct and psychologically different sets of characteristics, a confusion which is reflected in aptitude tests themselves. Some aptitudes are no different from the large group ability factors which have been discussed in the previous section. An obvious example is verbal aptitude. A person may be said to have verbal aptitude if he or she is quick to learn languages and speaks and writes with elegant fluency. The writer George Borrow, who claimed to be able to learn new languages in a week or so, is an obvious example of such an individual. This verbal aptitude, however, is identical with the ability factor verbal ability and verbal aptitude tests simply measure this factor.

The second group of aptitudes, however, is a collection of psychological traits, often embracing both personality and ability, which happen to be useful in a particular culture or society. The best example of this is clerical aptitude of which there is a variety of tests because clerks are valuable to many different commercial enterprises. Clerical aptitude requires speed and accuracy in computation and copying, conscientiousness in checking, orderliness and a resistance to boredom. Thus clerical aptitude tests must contain measures of all these variables.

As might be expected the two classes of aptitude have two different kinds of test. The first class are, as was mentioned above, simply tests of the major group factors. Verbal aptitude tests are measures of the verbal ability factor. Tests of spatial relations measure the spatial factor. These tests, therefore, are group factor ability tests under another name.

The second class of aptitude tests yield composite scores. These tests might be useful in certain occupations, and their value will be discussed in the next chapter, but it should be pointed out that it is psychometrically better practice to obtain separate scores for all the factors in a composite aptitude test rather than a combined score because a combined score may mean different things depending upon its particular combination. To exemplify from clerical aptitude two apparently identical scores might be composed of the highest score on accuracy with zero on neatness, for one score, and vice versa for the other.

One other point concerning aptitude tests needs to be made. At first sight it would appear that aptitude tests are ideal for occupational selection and appraisal. Thus verbal aptitude for journalists or barristers, mechanical aptitude for engineers and so on. Attractive as this seems, in fact they are not as valuable as might be expected. This is because, as was discussed in the opening section of this chapter, intelligence is a general ability factor which underlies all other abilities to a greater or lesser extent so that aptitude tests tend to measure general intelligence rather than the more specific aptitude. This problem will be discussed further in the next chapter when the use of aptitude tests in selection is examined.

# Personality tests

The definition of personality is a difficult matter in psychology. Indeed it has been said that there are as many definitions as personality theorists. Nevertheless from the psychometric viewpoint a definition is possible. Personality may be conceptualised in terms of temperament and dynamics. Temperament is concerned with how people do what they do, dynamics with why they do it. Strictly, temperament and dynamics are both aspects of personality, although in psychometrics tests of temperament are usually described as personality tests while tests of dynamics are thought of as motivational or interest tests. However, this is not a hard and fast distinction.

*Meaning of temperament.* Temperament may be thought of as a collection of traits describing behaviour. Washing up exemplifies temperamental traits with great clarity. Thus one person may do it methodically, lining up the plates and cutlery by type and size, washing and rinsing in separate bowls, using only green and organic washing up liquid. Another may do it at great speed, knocking the odd handle off a cup and chipping plates or worse. Yet another may leave them to soak, or simply leave them in the sink. All these different approaches to a mundane task reveal individual differences on a number of personality traits: orderliness, neatness, cleanliness, speed, carefulness, hope (that the washing up may just go away). Thus personality tests are concerned with these individual differences in temperamental traits.

As was the case with ability tests, but to an even greater extent, there is a severe problem of how many traits should be measured. As should be obvious there are as many traits, initially, as there are adjectives describing human behaviour. However, as was the case with test of ability, factor analysis has simplified the complexity and indicated the most important variables. These will be listed later in this chapter after the different types of personality test have been discussed.

## *Different types of personality test*

There are three kinds of personality test of which two are in common use while one is particularly suited to occupational selection and appraisal and will be discussed in more detail.

*Projective tests.* Projective tests usually consist of ambiguous stimuli, such as pictures of people in situations difficult to interpret, which subjects are required to describe. The theory underlying projective tests claims that individuals project onto the stimuli their own fears and conflicts which thus appear in their descriptions.

The difficulties with such tests are numerous and include: severe problems concerning the reliability of scoring since there are usually differences between scorers and between the same scorer on different occasions; further difficulties concerning the validity of these tests which has never been well supported; considerable skill and experience is needed before projective tests can be scored; almost all of them are individual tests and thus are time-consuming to give to large numbers of subjects. For all these reasons, as is obvious, projective tests are not regarded as useful for occupational psychology either for selection or appraisal. They have been mentioned here simply because one of the most famous psychological tests, known beyond the confines of psychology, is projective—the Rorschach Test. However even this test is subject to all the criticisms which have been discussed.

*Objective tests*. Objective tests are defined by Cattell, who is their main protagonist, as tests which can be objectively marked (thus improving reliability) and whose purpose cannot be guessed by subjects. This last would appear to be highly useful for selection since it makes faking extremely difficult. Faking is a problem as most individuals will attempt to make themselves appear as impressive and as suitable for the position as possible. This will be discussed below in relation to personality inventories.

Thus objective tests ought to be ideal for selection. That they are difficult if not impossible to fake is beyond dispute as a few examples will show.

(a) The slow line drawing tests. Subjects are required to draw a line as slowly as possible.
(b) Subjects are required to add some simple numbers which are set out among jokes.
(c) Good performance. Subjects are required to say whether a performance, eg learning to skate in three lessons, is good or not.

Most readers would not know what to put if they were being selected for a particular job, say a salesperson or a librarian. However the reason that these tests are little used is that there is no evidence that they are valid. Most of them have been put forward on an experimental basis but where attempts have been made to validate them they have not emerged well from the examination as is fully discussed in Kline (1992).

*Personality questionnaires or inventories*. For these reasons personality inventories, rather than these other types of personality tests, have been used for personnel selection. These consist of statements or questions about a subject's behaviour to which subjects have to respond, usually by "Yes" or "No" or "True" or "False". These are the tests which are most widely used in occupational psychology.

As was the case with tests of ability, the first difficulty concerns the variables to be measured. There could be as many personality tests as there are words to describe human behaviour—tests of bravery, ferocity, neatness and so on. This problem has been resolved by factor analysis and there is now fair agreement that five factors account for much of the variance in personality—the "big five": tough-mindedness, extroversion, anxiety, open-mindedness and conservatism. The personality inventories most suited to use in selection and appraisal will be discussed in Chapter 7.

Personality inventories have the following advantages.

(a) Inventories are easy to administer and can be given to large groups of subjects.
(b) They are easily and reliably scored. Many can be computer scored.
(c) It is possible to build up good norms for these tests or to develop relevant in-house norms.
(d) The best personality inventories have sound evidence in support of their validity. Some have specific research relating their scores to occupational success.

Personality inventories have the following disadvantages.

(a) They are easily faked. For example, few intending salespersons would admit to being shy or finding it difficult to talk to people. How to deal with this problem will be discussed in Chapter 7, as will the other difficulties described below.
(b) Response sets. The scores on personality inventories can be distorted by response sets which are stereotyped ways of responding to the items. There are two varieties of response set, acquiescence and social desirability.
    *Acquiescence.* This is the set to agree with items regardless of content. The best tests minimise this by having balanced scales with equal numbers of items scored "Yes" and "No" and by having items stated as clearly as possible.
    *Social desirability.* This is the tendency to respond to an item on the basis of how desirable it is. For example social desirability would rule out the items "I am a liar", "I am mean" or "I have no sense of humour". Clever item writing can minimise this problem.

Given all the difficulties with projective and objective tests, personality inventories are commonly used in personnel selection and appraisal despite their obvious problems. This is simply because, as shall be seen, there is clear evidence that they can improve selection.

## Interest and motivation tests

These tests are concerned with the dynamics of personality, the variables which account for why individuals act as they do. This is a field of psychological testing which has proved far more difficult than that of temperament and ability although one class of tests, interest tests, are used in occupational psychology.

There are various types of dynamic test and these are set out and described briefly below.

*State and mood tests.* States are transient, while traits are enduring. Moods are no different from states: that there are two words reflects nothing more than English usage. Because they are transient the measurement of states and moods plays virtually no part in occupational selection or appraisal and only two further points will be mentioned.

First, it might be useful to measure anxiety as a trait *and* as a state (since applicants will be differentially made anxious by the selection procedures, thereby affecting their performance). Notice that anxiety can be both a state and a trait.

Second, although anger is a transient mood it might be useful to know how often an individual became angry or went into any other state which might affect performance at work.

*Interest tests.* Interest tests are extensively used in occupational psychology since on simple, common sense grounds it is to be expected that people will do more effectively jobs in which they are interested rather than uninterested or ones which they actually hate.

The majority of interest tests have been developed with occupational selection in mind and they cover the main interest categories, eg adventure, agriculture, merchandising, military, musical, social services and teaching. Tests which will be discussed in Chapter 8 vary in the number of interests which they measure, ranging from about 20 downwards. In addition some interest tests attempt to find the occupation or job in which the subject is interested.

The items in these interest tests resemble those of personality inventories consisting of statements, or sometimes actual job titles, which subjects have to rank or state their degree of liking or interest.

The difficulty with many of these interest tests is that their correlations with job satisfaction or success are somewhat small and in some cases no larger than the correlation with the simple question "What job would you like?". The other major difficulty lies in the fact that many of these tests are atheoretical but rely on the fact that the scales can discriminate the occupants of a particular job from controls. This is fine until the nature of a job changes, as has occurred in many cases with the advent of robotics and computers. Furthermore it means that results from America cannot be applied in other countries where jobs of the same name may be very different.

## Other tests

The vast majority of psychological tests fall within the four categories which have been discussed in this chapter so far. Other categories of tests, such as neuro-psychological tests, special clinical tests or attainment tests, have no part to play in occupational selection and appraisal and will not be discussed here.

From this discussion of the types of psychological tests it is clear that ability, aptitude, personality and interest tests all have a part to play in occupational psychology. Just what that part is will be discussed in the next chapters of this book.

# Chapter 6
# Use of Ability Tests in Personnel Work

The place of ability tests both for appraisal and selection is examined below. Under the term *ability tests* will be included aptitude tests, which, as was demonstrated in the previous chapter, are essentially tests of ability even though some are confounded with personality.

## Intelligence Tests

Intelligence is one of the most pervasive psychological variables. There is virtually no aspect of behaviour in which intelligence does not play a part. Kline (1991) in *Intelligence: The Psychometric View* summarised the evidence relevant to educational and occupational psychology. Ghiselli (1966), in a famous monograph, showed that intelligence test scores were the best single predictor of job success of all variables, the average correlation being .3. This may not sound high but it is across the whole spectrum of jobs and was based upon 10,000 investigations. What this means is that if a personnel manager had to select individuals for unspecified jobs the intelligence test would be helpful. This is almost certainly the only test which could ease this impossible task. Similar conclusions can be drawn from the work of Vernon and Parry (1949) who organised personnel selection in the British Forces during the Second World War. Here again the importance of intelligence in the selection process was attested, just as was the weakness of the interview.

Of course the personnel manager is never required to select individuals for unknown jobs and this is where the role of other abilities comes into play. What abilities these are depends upon the job itself (see Chapter 4 where the selection of the right test was discussed). What variables are salient to a job should be ascertained from some kind of job description.

However, before simply relying on job descriptions to know which abilities to test a few points concerning the role of intelligence in job selection need to be made.

Certain posts require their holders to be intelligent if the duties are to be adequately performed. Administrative civil servants, the directors of large and complex organisations, come to mind. However if a correlation between intelligence and performance at these jobs were to be computed it would almost certainly be small. This is due to the fact that the holders of these posts are all highly intelligent, having, in the case of the civil service, been selected on the criterion of high intelligence. This is a demonstration of the fact that if a variable is *restricted in range* the correlation with other variables is inevitably lowered, although it does not mean that it is unimportant in success. Imagine, for example, that all the civil servants had IQs of either 131 or 132. In that case it is obvious that the correlation of intelligence with their performance would be negligible. In the real life instance the effect is similar. All the civil servants are sufficiently intelligent to perform the job well, hence other variables must account for individual differences.

The point of this example is to illustrate the dangers of uninformed interpretation of correlation coefficients. A similar lowering of correlation is found between intelligence and university performance for much the same reason. What the correlation might be can be envisaged in the case where a true cross-section of the community, including subnormals, were allowed to take university exams. The correlation between IQ and performance would be considerable.

Thus the fact that the correlation between intelligence and success in some occupations is low does not mean that intelligence is not a salient factor. It would only do so if the sample were drawn from the whole range of possible scores. Of course if the correlation is high then it does imply that intelligence is salient to success.

*If correlations between IQ and occupational success are thus restricted, how is it possible to argue that intelligence is an important variable in such success?* This is a most reasonable question since it is obvious that in "real life" there never is a cross-section of the population in any one job. All correlations between success and intelligence are reduced. There are two answers to the above question.

(a) Job analysis. Careful job analysis should reveal which occupations demand intelligence and which do not.
(b) The mean intelligence test scores of different occupational groups should be compared. This indicates which groups are intelligent and where the results are consonant with job analysis there can be little doubt that intelligence is a salient variable.

This second proviso is important. For example in the 1930s in Great Britain, testing the IQ of different occupational groups revealed that engine drivers were very high scorers. This was not because high intelligence was necessary for a good driver but as a result of a number of social factors. Engine driving was one of the safest and best jobs for those who had little education and at that time there was poor access to education for the working class. The job, therefore, was highly competitive, and the more intelligent railwaymen obtained the posts.

The engine drivers typified what was not at all uncommon before the war. In many posts where intelligence was no direct advantage intelligent individuals, who had for reasons of money and social class been denied any but the briefest education, could be found. Such people did these jobs remarkably efficiently, often discovering short cuts and methods which were superior to standard procedures. This greatly added to the efficiency of their organisations, although from the viewpoint of job holders their talents were wasted and underpaid.

Thus in one sense to have intelligent people in jobs below their level of ability may be a good thing for the organisation. The personnel manager even when selecting for posts where intelligence is not essential would do well to take the most intelligent subjects—all other things being equal and taking into account the possibility that intelligent people might become bored and dissatisfied.

It might be argued that where posts demand high educational and professional qualifications it is somewhat pointless to bother with intelligence testing. Indeed it was argued above that intelligence was correlated with academic success so that in these cases all the applicants will be intelligent. Although this is so it does not follow that intelligence testing is redundant.

To obtain academic and professional qualifications demands intelligence, application and determination. Accountancy and legal examinations, for example, throw considerable burdens on memory and demand hard work to pass. Thus attainment is a function of hard work and intelligence. Now it is quite clear that the subject who has managed to pass examinations only with the greatest effort will find it more difficult to adapt to changes in legislation and methods of working and to deal with novel problems than will the intelligent person whose qualifications are the same. It would be absurd to take on the less intelligent applicant. These same arguments apply to most professions where knowledge and procedures change. In brief, intelligence, because it involves the capacity to master new things, is always a valuable attribute.

There is a common stereotype of the brilliant but mad professor who in any responsible position, despite his or her intelligence, would be disastrous, unable to exist beyond the ivory tower. This has persuaded some employers to fear the brilliant person. Even if there is some truth in this picture, it should not be used to avoid the most intelligent applicants. The fact is that there is not an inevitable link between high intelligence and absent-mindedness or whatever else might be used in describing this particular stereotype. If the link occurs, and it can usually be recognised without tests, then the person can be turned down. This highlights the point that intelligence, although a highly salient trait in occupational success, is only one among many. However if there are no other reasons to turn down a highly intelligent applicant, this high intelligence should be regarded as an asset, not a possible disadvantage. In brief all other things being equal the most intelligent applicants should be selected. This is a sound rule for occupational psychology, but there is an exception.

The only situation where high intelligence may be relatively disadvantageous is in posts where the work is monotonous and intelligent subjects may grow bored and perform poorly. Two examples of monotonous work illustrate the point.

*Football pool checkers.* Many years ago before the advent of automation it was found by one of the largest football pool operators that quick and accurate pool checking was hindered by high intelligence. These subjects became bored and slowed up or made errors. Two points should be noted about this case. First low intelligence was not advantageous either. It was simply that above a certain point on the intelligence scale boredom intervened. There was still a positive correlation between intelligence and success. Secondly there were no opportunities in this job for intelligent people to do it better and thus obtain job satisfaction in that way, which is somewhat unusual.

*Selection of production line car workers.* Working on the production line of car factories is notoriously taxing and not highly interesting. However, it is noteworthy that in some of the most modern plants there are possibilities for the more intelligent worker. Thus the methods are not fixed and workers are encouraged to produce innovations in procedure which will benefit the company. In one particular plant some of the innovations have been highly successful and used throughout the world. This means that even though the job is essentially boring the intelligent worker will be more successful and be more satisfied since even here there are opportunities to utilise intelligence.

There is one final argument which, in this writer's opinion, on its own makes intelligence testing a vital part of selection procedures. There is clear evidence that intelligence is correlated with the speed of mastering the new (Jensen, 1980). Thus, for example in the early stages of learning music, the highly intelligent individual will quickly pick up the notation even if not musically gifted, although later he or she may be overtaken by those more interested in music and more prepared to practise. This applies to all fields.

Now in most jobs during the lifetime of a workforce there are inevitably considerable changes of procedures and practices, none more marked than the invasion of computing into the workplace. The more intelligent a workforce, the more easily it can adapt to change. The luddite is usually low on g, general ability.

From this it is quite clear that on rational grounds quite apart from job descriptions, the intelligence test is virtually always valuable in selection. It should be routinely administered.

*Rationale of using other ability tests.* This can be a brief discussion since the reasons for using such tests are obvious. Thus if a job demands high verbal ability it is clear that a test of verbal ability should be part of the selection procedure. However what form such a test should take is not so clear-cut. A few examples will clarify this problem.

It is obvious from job descriptions that actuaries or statisticians require high mathematical ability and that engineers require considerable mathematical and spatial ability. However applicants for these jobs would possess the relevant professional qualifications. Thus they would possess sufficient ability to do the job. Furthermore, unlike the more general intelligence, these would be abilities specific to the actual jobs. Hence the only tests which would be valuable for such applicants would be high level tests of these abilities. In fact these do not exist. Where high level abilities are required and where applicants possess relevant qualifications demanding these abilities it is usually not sensible to attempt to test for abilities. The qualifications themselves must be regarded as adequate measures.

This leads to a general point about ability testing. The more specific abilities should only be tested where the jobs involve something new to applicants and where their qualifications are not relevant. A typical example of this is in the field of computing, where spatial ability and numerical reasoning would appear to be highly relevant. However as Cook (1990) has shown, computer aptitude tests of this type do predict well but in effect are little more than tests of non–verbal intelligence or fluid ability.

An even clearer example of this can be seen in army selection where the applicants have a minimum of educational qualifications, so that there is little guide to their real abilities. Here intelligence and aptitude tests can be useful since they will indicate a bias to verbal or numerical ability which may be useful in selection.

In other words, as was pointed out in Chapter 5, the utility in practical selection of tests of ability and aptitude is often less than might be expected, because essentially they are measures of intelligence, and add in little over and above intelligence tests.

It can be concluded that ability and aptitude tests are most valuable when there is no other indication of the ability of the applicants. Here they may give useful insights into the nature of an applicant's abilities but the pervasive influence of intelligence, a general ability, reduces the information which may be obtained with them. They tend to measure intelligence.

With candidates who have obtained the requisite professional or academic qualifications for high level jobs where abilities are necessary it is difficult to find better measures than the qualifications themselves. In brief aptitude and ability tests add little to what may be learned from an intelligence test.

# Useful intelligence and ability tests in occupational selection and appraisal

*Raven's Matrices* (Raven, 1965). There are three versions of this test:
  (a) Standard Matrices. Age range: 6½ to 65 years. Subjects: Average ability. Time: 45 Minutes.
  (b) Coloured Matrices. This will not be further described since it is for adults of low or impaired ability and is thus unsuited for occupational work.
  (c) Advanced Matrices. Age range: 11 to adult. Subjects: Above average ability—graduates and those with professional qualifications or those leaving school with a good academic record. Time: 40–60 minutes.

The Standard and Advanced Matrices are highly similar tests, differing only in their level of difficulty and I shall discuss them as one test.

*Variable measured.* Fluid ability $g_f$. Raven's Matrices, a non-verbal intelligence test, is regarded as the best single test of fluid ability. It measures the basic innate ability of the individual and so is particularly suitable for subjects whose education or English has been limited. It is also highly valuable in work with arts graduates whose performance on verbal intelligence tests is often boosted by their studies. Subjects who score highly on this test are likely to be good at mastering new problems.

*Type of item.* Non-verbal. Items consist of sequences of patterns. Subjects have to choose the next one in the sequence. This involves working out the rules governing the sequence and applying the rule to select the correct response. As is obvious, such items are novel to most people and this test is a great leveller of social class differences.

*Reliability and validity.* This is a highly reliable and valid test of intelligence, as is demonstrated in countless studies.

*Norms.* Although new supplementary norms were produced in 1982 this is the weakest aspect of the test. However, it is not fatal to its use in the occupational field since there is no question that high performance, especially on the advanced version, represents high intelligence. House norms can also be developed when required.

This is certainly one of the best tests of intelligence and is particularly suited for subjects whose first language is not English.

With highly educated subjects there is little point in giving a verbal intelligence test, a non-verbal test such as Raven's Matrices will certainly be more revealing. However where applicants for positions are less educated such as in taking on workers for a large, new factory, a verbal intelligence test can be useful. Raven (1965) produced just such a quick measure:

*The Mill-Hill Vocabulary Scale*. This is the verbal equivalent of the Standard Matrices—to be used with average subjects.

*Items*. Vocabulary.

*Reliability and validity*. These are high. Vocabulary is the best single test for crystallised intelligence.

*Norms*. As for Standard Matrices.

For a quick measure of verbal intelligence the Mill-Hill Vocabulary Scale is efficient and effective, although a longer verbal intelligence scale should be given, if, for some reason, it is essential to measure this crystallised ability.

Such a measure might be required, for example, if workers were needed for expansion into Europe and where intensive language training was to be given for engineers or salespeople. Then a verbal intelligence test would be valuable. Two intelligence tests are briefly described below. One is purely verbal, the other tests both aspects of intelligence.

*Watson-Glaser Critical Thinking Appraisal* (Watson and Glaser, 1964).

*Subjects*. This test is designed for graduate recruitment and management selection.

*Items*. Drawing inferences from facts; recognising assumptions implicit in statements; drawing deductions from facts; interpretation of statements and evaluation of arguments.

*Reliability and validity*. This is fine and it correlates highly with other good intelligence tests.

This is an excellent test of verbal intelligence, crystallised ability. It differs from other intelligence tests in that it avoids short items but has longer passages of English to test reasoning. It is only suited to high level personnel but it gives good predictions for success on training courses.

*The Alice Heim Intelligence Tests*. The final intelligence tests to be described are those of Alice Heim and her colleagues (Heim et al, 1970, 1974).

These measure crystallised and fluid intelligence and are clearly valuable where both must be tested. There are various versions for subjects of different ability and training. These are set out below.

47

AH2 and AH3. These are the tests for adults of average ability. AH2 and AH3 are parallel forms.

AH6 is the test for the graduate level adult. There are two versions, one for scientists and engineers, the other for arts students.

Crystallised intelligence is measured by verbal reasoning items (analogies, following instructions, categorisation and working out complex family relationships) and by numerical reasoning items (problems, analogies and the four basic rules, involving timetables and the speed of vehicles).

Fluid intelligence is measured by non-verbal analogies and categorisation but with diagrammatic material, as well as with matrices-like items.

*Reliability and validity.* These are reliable tests with sound evidence for validity both for fluid and crystallised ability.

All the AH tests are useful measures of the two intelligence factors. If measures of both fluid and crystallised ability are needed these are simple and effective tests.

*Other tests of ability.* As should be clear from the discussion of aptitude and ability tests in the previous chapter, the value of these is limited in occupational selection on account of the fact that abilities are correlated so that ultimately they tend to measure intelligence. For this reason the tests are listed with a brief description only. The value of these tests in occupational psychology lies, in any case, only with subjects whose educational attainment is low, thus giving no indication of aptitude, but who are applying for posts demanding some kind of further training. They are thus of some value with older people who may have missed out on education and are retraining. However at best these tests can indicate only rather general trends, eg numerical or scientific rather than arts abilities.

The *Comprehensive Ability Battery* (Hakstian and Cattell, 1976). This measures 20 of the most important ability factors. To give the whole test is hopelessly cumbersome for occupational selection or appraisal. However, if a job description indicates that any of these ability factors are salient to the position, the scales in this test are reasonably valid and reliable. The abilities measured are:

| | | | |
|---|---|---|---|
| 1 | Verbal ability | 7 | Flexibility of closure |
| 2 | Numerical ability | 8 | Rote memory |
| 3 | Spatial ability | 9 | Mechanical ability |
| 4 | Speed of closure | 10 | Memory span |
| 5 | Perceptual speed and accuracy | 11 | Meaningful memory |
| 6 | Inductive reasoning | 12 | Spelling |

| 13 | Aesthetic judgement | 17 | Originality |
|----|---------------------|----|-------------|
| 14 | Spontaneous flexibility | 18 | Auditory ability |
| 15 | Ideational fluency | 19 | Aiming |
| 16 | Word fluency | 20 | Representational drawing |

The CAB was developed to measure the main ability factors. Although they are correlated, the correlations are not so high as to render the test simply a measure of the two intelligence factors, although these do account for much of the variance. However with the two aptitude tests most widely used in America, the Differential Aptitude Test (DAT) and the General Aptitude Test Battery (GATB), this is not the case. In these tests the scales are highly correlated and these tests are not differential as has been discussed in detail by Kline (1992). For these reasons neither of these tests is recommended for occupational selection and appraisal.

The DAT measures the following variables: verbal reasoning, abstract reasoning, numerical ability, clerical aptitude, mechanical reasoning, space relations, spelling and grammar. This is a test for the age range 12 to 17 years and subjects who are above average tend to find some of the scales too easy.

The GATB measures: general intelligence, verbal, numerical and spatial ability, form perception, clerical perception, motor coordination, finger dexterity and manual dexterity.

It should be noted that this test departs from the pencil and paper routine and uses apparatus to measure finger and manual dexterity. However, despite the face validity of these tests their correlations with engineering skill, although positive, are low. In general, however, this test again measures little more than intelligence.

As must be now clear there is little reason to use aptitude tests since in general they measure little more than crystallised and fluid ability. Hence it is more sensible to measure these variables directly. If some specific ability seems to be required in most selection situations it is necessary also that the applicants have reached a satisfactory level of attainment so that even if ability tests were available they would not necessarily be useful. In general, tests of intelligence are the most useful in occupational selection and if the most intelligent applicants (other things being equal) are selected performance should improve.

# Chapter 7
# Use of Personality Tests in Personnel Work

In Chapter 5 the different types of personality tests were described and discussed: personality questionnaires or inventories; projective tests and objective tests. As was made clear in that chapter, projective tests are not suited to personnel selection because, generally, they are individual measures which are time consuming, require considerable training if they are to be interpreted and, finally, there is little evidence supporting their validity. Objective tests are experimental and although they may prove useful, when the relevant investigations are carried out, at present it would not be rational to use them. Thus, this chapter will be devoted to the use of personality inventories (a term which includes questionnaires) in personnel selection and appraisal.

## Rationale for the use of personality inventories

Intuitively, without any special knowledge of psychology, it is obvious that personality differences are implicated in job satisfaction and success. For example a highly imaginative, sensitive and unconventional person could never be satisfactory in any position requiring conformity and discipline such as the army or police. Similarly for sales positions certain personal qualities are advantageous, eg sociability, thick-skinnedness and so on. These are quite different from those necessary for a librarian or statistician.

These claims arise from observation. In fact there is now considerably more objective evidence that personality differences do, indeed, play an important role in job satisfaction, which is usually related to good performance. Herriot (1989) and Kline (1992) contain discussions of some of this evidence.

In Chapter 4, Selecting the Right Tests, it was pointed out that the demands of jobs in terms of psychological characteristics could be assessed in a variety

51

of ways, by job analysis and questionnaire, for example. All these methods indicate clearly, in support of everyday observation, that personality tests should be included in personnel selection and appraisal.

In brief, it can be confidently asserted that personality variables are implicated in job satisfaction and success such that any rational selection procedure and system of appraisal must utilise the best measures of personality available—personality inventories.

# Using personality inventories in personnel selection

There are three basic approaches to the use of personality tests in personnel work and these are set out below. An assumption of these methods, which underlies the use of all psychological tests in occupational selection, is that there is some ideal specification, in terms of psychological characteristics, for each position.

## *Matching*

In the matching method the scores on personality tests of each applicant are matched with the scores of occupants of the relevant position. For example, if a cost accountant is required then each applicant's score is matched up to the scores of cost accountants. Of course it is possible to do this with a whole range of test scores, including personality, aptitude and ability and motivation and interests, but the method is particularly appropriate for personality measures which often yield a profile of scores. The individual who fits the profile most closely is the one to choose, at least in respect of personality. It is possible to obtain a statistical match, for each applicant, by using the profile index which is set out in the *Handbook to the 16PF Test* (Cattell et al, 1970), which is described later in this chapter.

There are several important points which should be made about this matching method so that its problems and advantages may be understood.

*Samples of the groups used for matching.* With this method it is essential that the groups to which applicants are matched are representative of the occupation. If this is not the case the method is bound to be riddled with error.

In practice, this means that samples must be large and well chosen, as was discussed in Chapter 3 on test norms. However, this is often not the case since it is difficult to obtain adequate samples and before using this method it is advisable to check up on the relevant normative group.

*Relevance of the matching groups.* Since there are so many different jobs it is obvious that in some instances there will be no relevant group. This method cannot then be used. However, often there may be a normative set of scores derived from a job which is similar but not identical to what is required. Here it makes sense to use the information, but caution in interpreting the results must be advised.

This is particularly important where the normative group is American (and many of the best tests are American) but the selection is for posts in Great Britain. Cross-cultural comparison of occupational scores can be hazardous since the requirements for jobs of the same title in different countries may be different. Lawyers are an obvious case in point but because the cultural climate in the two countries is so different even relatively similar jobs are not completely comparable.

*Using in-house norms.* In-house norms form the best basis for comparison provided that these are derived from a substantial sample and that the requirements of the post have not changed over the years. Computers, for example, have changed radically the demands of those working in stock control. In-house norms, gathered over a number of years, could be misleading.

*Profiles becoming out of date.* The demands of jobs alter, often as new technology becomes available. This means that the profiles used for matching, even when the job appears to be precisely relevant, may be inappropriate. Ideally profiles should be regularly updated.

*Are job applicants necessarily suited to their positions?* A possible objection to the matching procedure arises from this question. The method appears to assume that, by some miraculous fortune, people work in the jobs most suited to them. Would this were the case. Indeed, given the haphazard ways in which jobs are obtained and the inefficiency of most selection systems, and, in Great Britain at least, the ubiquity of the old boy network, it might be argued that a selection system based upon matching was bound to fail.

While these points have a degree of truth, it must be realised that the vast majority of job occupants are reasonably efficient and can tolerate their posts. If neither were true in the majority of instances, their organisations would fail. Thus a group of accountants, for example, are far more likely to possess the characteristics required by accountants than are any other occupational group. This is a sufficient basis for the matching method. The method does not imply that occupants ideally suit their posts.

*Lack of norms.* It has to be said that the majority of personality tests do not possess sufficient normative data to allow the matching method to be used in a large variety of jobs. Even where norms are presented in many cases they are imperfect, although better than nothing.

The conclusions, from the viewpoint of practical personnel selection, are simple and clear. They are summarised below.

(a) The matching method, in its precise form, using a profile index, should only be used where there are excellent norms fitting the job and derived from a large sample. This means that it will be used only on rare occasions.

(b) Usually the most sensible use of the profiles on personality tests is to note the high and low scores and regard all applicants with such a pattern as being suitable in terms of personality for the post. This is a far less rigorous use of the norms but in so doing it does not require the same precision of measurement. Such a procedure essentially produces a list which would then be sifted through against other criteria.

## The regression method

The 16PF test exemplifies this approach to the use of tests, which can be highly effective provided that the empirical studies, from which the regression equations are derived, utilised good samples. In this method regression equations are computed between the personality test scores and success at the job. These equations should be contained in the manual to the test.

*Meaning of regression equations.* In multiple regression the overall correlation between a set of scores and a criterion score will have been computed: to take a concrete example, the multiple correlation between the 16PF scales and success at accountancy. In multiple correlation not only is this multiple correlation given, but, even more important, the beta weights for each scale are computed. These indicate the importance of the scale in the overall correlation. Thus in selecting accountants the scores on each scale multiplied by their beta weights constitute an applicant's score. The higher this score the more suited to accountancy he or she is. The larger the multiple correlation the more confidence can be placed in this overall score. Similar scores can be computed for other professions given that the regression equations are set out in the test manual.

As with the matching method a number of points are salient to the regression method. Some are identical to those made above so that they will simply be listed without further comment.

(a) The sampling must be representative of the occupation. As with the first method the sampling must be satisfactory or the results will be misleading.

(b) The relevance of groups. Again it is important that the groups are relevant to the posts for which applicants are being selected.

(c) In-house norms. These are highly satisfactory provided that the numbers are sufficient and the psychological demands of the job have not changed.

(d) The regression equations must not be out of date. As with the profiles in the matching method, the regression equations must be derived from recent occupants of the posts.

(e) The beta weights, on account of the computations involved in regression, maximise chance effects. Thus they are likely to vary from sample to sample, although with very large samples fluctuation is reduced. However, with samples of less than 100 correction of the beta weights should always be made.

(f) Although it is beyond the scope of this book to discuss how success at a job should be measured, in many occupations this is a problem. If the criterion in a regression equation is unreliable or invalid, the resulting beta weights are bound to be riddled with error. This is a considerable difficulty with the regression method.

Of course, the ease with which success in a particular job can be measured varies considerably. A few examples will illustrate the difficulties involved. There is a relatively clear criterion for the success of a salesperson—volume of sales. However even this would be a gross oversimplification. In comparing sales of cars through a network of dealers across Great Britain, there would be large regional differences, based upon their affluence. However there would be sources of variation beyond this. One outlet might be close to a rival who was supremely efficient, another might be close to one which was poor and yet another might be on its own. In a good measure of occupational success or efficiency these factors should be taken into account.

It is obvious that even in a relatively simple case, such as salespersons, the criterion of success is not clear-cut. In most positions, however, the problems are far more acute. It is difficult to imagine, for example, a good criterion measure for a personnel manager, and some occupations, such as teaching, have defeated most attempts at assessment. This is largely because success at most jobs is multi-dimensional involving a complex of activities. Often the simplest solution, ratings by an immediate supervisor, may be as good a single criterion as can be obtained.

From this discussion it can be concluded that the problem of the criterion of success is a major source of difficulty with the regression method.

If all the problems associated with the regression method have been resolved it can be useful because it involves success at the occupation, not simply membership. Unfortunately the majority of personality tests do not have sufficient occupational data to enable the regression method to be used in a wide variety of selection situations. Although the 16PF test has a large number of samples, many of these are too small to place much confidence in them, although they are better than nothing. Clearly the regression method is best when used with in-house ratings of success.

In practical use, as was argued above, a score can be obtained for each candidate by adding the scale scores multiplied by their beta weights. The candidate with the highest score is thus the most likely to be successful at the job.

The strict and rigorous use of these methods, selecting candidates with the highest pattern profile similarity coefficient or the highest score on the regression method, could only be justified where the tests were of extremely high validity and reliability, where the profiles and regression weights were derived from large and representative samples, where the measures of success were reliable and valid and where the methods had shown themselves to be effective.

Unfortunately none of these conditions can be met in practice. This description of the two approaches has been included to represent the ideal, to which occupational psychologists must strive. As has been argued elsewhere (Kline, 1992), this involves the compilation over the years of an encyclopaedia of job specifications where the regression weights for success and occupational profiles of large numbers of jobs could be found.

However, the current use of personality tests cannot be so rigorous. Their scores must be combined with other sources of information and how this may be done is described in Chapters 11 and 12.

In the opening section of this chapter it was suggested that there were three methods of using personality tests. The description of the third method, using tests suggested by job analysis, can be brief since job analysis and description has already been discussed in Chapter 4, and the rationale of the method is obvious. It is the use of tests suggested by common sense.

## *Personality tests and job analysis and description*

As was pointed out in Chapter 4 the description and analysis of jobs can be done by observation and minute description, by interviews with the occupants and by questionnaire. From task description and analysis the psychological demands of a post can be set out. Personality tests can be used in occupational selection on this basis. Thus if job analysis suggests that a stable extrovert is required for a particular post, then the best tests of these variables can be used. Clearly this method depends upon the adequacy of the job analysis and the validity of the tests.

Of course, this method can be the basis of selecting all types of psychological test, not simply tests of personality. Batteries of tests, selected by job analysis, must be validated. Thus it is essential to show that the tests improve selection.

Although the correlations between occupational success and personality tests scores may be small, in the region of .3 in many cases, this does not mean that the tests are of little value. The point is that without tests selection would be random. Even small correlations, therefore, represent an improvement. This is especially true if the variance which they account for is separate from that accounted by ability tests as is the case with personality tests. Thus it can be argued that despite the small correlations personality tests are worth using in occupational selection.

There are other problems with personality tests in selection.

*Faking.* Faking is a problem in personality tests used in the selection context. However, most tests contain a lie scale, which will screen out those who are attempting to fake their responses and if it is made clear to applicants that faking can be detected this usually reduces the problem.

However, it should be pointed out that if a test has proved itself useful or valid in selection, this is evidence that its scores are not undermined by faking and thus this difficulty can be ignored.

*Ipsative scores.* In Chapter 4 ipsative scores (where forced choices or ranking are involved) were discussed and it was pointed out that these were unsuited to the development of norms or to multivariate statistical analyses thus making ipsatively scored tests suited only to appraisal rather than selection.

*Personality tests in appraisal: career development.* This use of personality tests is quite different from that in selection. In career development the results are discussed with the subject and the meaning and implications of the scores are explored. Here the precise scores and correlations with criteria are of little significance. All that is necessary are broad categories such as average, or above average. Thus a picture of the subject's personality can be built up, and in the light of this career possibilities can be discussed. Of course, other tests such as abilities and motivation would also be used.

Sometimes subjects may feel that the depiction of their personality from the test scores is incorrect. This can lead to interesting insights both into the test and sometimes the subject and can be highly fruitful.

In appraisal there is far less use of the actual scores than there is in selection. Indeed the tests form the basis of discussion. For this reason ipsative tests come into their own since the rankings made by subjects can be discussed and their significance can be discovered. Indeed because of the emphasis on the discussion of the test in appraisal it may not matter so much which personality test is used, since the relevance and meaning of any set of items can be a valuable starting point for the appraisal.

*Useful personality tests in personnel selection.* It would be impossible to list all the personality tests which might be useful in selection. However, readers should be able to select the useful tests for themselves, against the criteria for good tests which have been discussed throughout this book—reliability, validity, properly constituted norms and ideally some specific occupationally relevant results such as the scores of different occupational groups or correlations with occupational success.

*Differences between factored and other personality tests.* There are two kinds of personality inventory. One type is produced through factor analysis and the scales here are unidimensional, measuring clear factors which in the best tests have been identified and validated against external criteria. These are the best tests to use in personnel selection because as data are built up over the years such tests can yield theoretical insights into the nature of occupational success and satisfaction. This is because externally validated factors have psychological meaning.

However some personality tests are purely empirical: items are chosen for a scale if they can make relevant discriminations. For example the MMPI depression scale consists of items which can discriminate depressives from other groups. Such scales, even if they can make occupational discriminations, are not recommended because they have no psychological meaning, and as jobs change such tests become inefficient.

To conclude this chapter, therefore, the factor analytic personality inventories which have the best evidence for validity are listed below. Those which I list measure the factors which were described in Chapter 5, as measuring the most important in the temperamental sphere.

1. The Eysenck Personality Questionnaire, EPQ (Eysenck & Eysenck, 1975). This is unquestionably one of the best personality inventories available. It forms a benchmark measure for extroversion and neuroticism.

Variables measured. Extroversion, neuroticism, psychotism (tough-mindedness) and L, a lie scale, concerned with social desirability.

Items. 90 items of the yes/no variety. It takes about 20 minutes to complete and is suitable for subjects of average ability or above.

Norms. It has good population norms and the scores of a variety of occupational groups.

Comments. This is one of the best validated personality inventories. There are literally hundreds of studies supporting its validity. Its main value is in providing excellent measures of the three largest personality factors which certainly play a part in occupational success and satisfaction. From the viewpoint of personnel selection its slight weakness is that these are broad factors. This has been addressed in a more recent version of the test published in 1992. This has improved measures of P and narrower factors of impulsivity and venturesomeness which have been shown to be important personality factors. This new version of the test should certainly be the one to choose in personnel work, if these variables are judged to be salient.

2. Cattell's 16PF Test. (Cattell et al, 1970). Cattell has been one of the main

protagonists of factor analysis in the construction of personality inventories and this 16PF test is still one of the most widely used inventories in personnel work.

Variables. It measures the 16 factors claimed by Cattell to underlie the variance of personality. However recent work has called these into question, as has been fully discussed in Kline (1992). However there are extensive occupational norms and profiles for this test, mainly of American origin, although many British norms are also available (see Herriot, 1989). At the second order Cattell's factors are not unlike the big five discussed in Chapter 5—extroversion, anxiety, open-mindedness, tough-mindedness and conventionality. Because of the vast amount of occupational research with this test, despite the problems, it can be a useful instrument.

Forms. There are various forms of the test which are claimed to be parallel although the correlations between them are not as high as is desirable.

Items. 187 trichotomous items, with a warning to use the middle category as little as possible.

Time. 45 minutes to complete.

Final comments. As was indicated in our discussion of variables, there are doubts concerning the primary factors of this test although they will discriminate among occupational groups. Furthermore the reliability of these scales is less than desirable. Yet, despite all these difficulties, because of the occupational work that has been done with these scales it can be meaningful to use them. At the second order especially the results are more robust. If used with care, and if validated for the particular job involved, it can be cautiously recommended, if the EPQ seems too broad.

These are the two most famous factored tests. There is a huge number of other tests which I cannot list in a chapter of this length. In my *Handbook of Psychological Testing* (Kline, 1992) I describe a considerable number of them in detail. To conclude this chapter, therefore, I shall make a number of points about the selection of suitable personality inventories and simply mention a few possible tests.

1   Tests with a large number of variables are probably not valid—given the evidence that there are at the most five large factors accounting for personality variance.

2   Tests which claim to measure typologies, such as the Myers-Briggs Inventory (Briggs and Myers, 1970) are unlikely to be valid since there is little evidence that human beings can be classified into types and, in addition, Jungian theory which forms the basis of this test has little claim to validity. What this test might measure is discussed fully in Kline (1992).

3   The best test of the big five is that developed by the main proponents

of this position. This is the Neo Personality Inventory (Costa and McCrae, 1988). However this is an American test and for Great Britain validating studies are required.

Conclusions. From this chapter it is clear that for selection, personality inventories can be used with advantage, the correlations with occupational success being modest but positive and accounting for variance different from that explainable in terms of ability. The EPQ is an outstanding test of three of the main personality factors. However, where more detailed measurement is required, the newer version of this test and the 16PF test are probably best despite the problems with this latter measure. Other personality tests may be useful for specific purposes but care should be taken with tests claiming to measure a large number of personality variables or to allocate people into groups.

In general personality inventories are not as yet sufficiently validated and the necessary data are not collected to use them as they should ideally be used, as instruments of which the scores can be trusted and inserted into regression equations or matching profiles. At present, as will be described in Chapters 11 and 12, their scores must be interpreted alongside and in the light of other information.

# Chapter 8
# Use of Interest and Motivation Tests in Personnel Work

It should be obvious that the measurement of interest and motivation would be useful in personnel selection and appraisal and that therefore there is little point in making the case. Clearly people work better and are happier in jobs in which they are interested rather than uninterested. A consideration of the meaning of interest suggests that this common sense intuition is correct. Thus a person may be said to be interested in a task if he or she spends a long time working at it voluntarily, and devotes money and effort towards it. In other words interest is normally inferred from behaviour. Most people who are interested in something are well aware that this is the case and can tell other people. However the simple question "Are you interested in X?" is probably not useful in selection or appraisal because people may lie. Thus if an applicant wants a job working with cars it is unlikely that he or she would claim to be uninterested. Even so it is worthy of note that a simple question relating to interests seems to discriminate occupational groups as well as one of the best known and complex interest tests, the Strong Vocational Interest Blank, which will be discussed later in this section, as Katz (1972) demonstrated.

Two conclusions for personnel selection and appraisal may be drawn from this discussion of the meaning of interest.

First, it is indeed likely that interests are a good predictor of job performance, if other variables from the fields of personality and ability are equal. This is simply because the interested person, by definition, enjoys the work and would do it for its own sake.

The point that personality and ability must not be ignored in the consideration of interest is important. Thus in any regression equation with the criterion occupational success, it means that interests can be expected to play a part distinct from ability and personality. This must be the case since the correlations between

61

these three classes of variable are small. Thus interests, even if their correlation with occupational success are not high, are still useful because they account for different variance compared with personality and ability measures.

It is not necessary to be a statistician to see why this should be so. To take the example of cars, again, there are plenty of young people who find them interesting but not all these are capable of becoming engineers. This is due to the fact that they lack the requisite mathematical and general abilities. Not all, at a lower level, would make good production line workers due to temperamental differences. Extroverts are likely to find production line work highly aversive.

There is one further point on the maintenance of interest which should be noted here. This is discussed only briefly because it lies outside the bounds of a book on occupational testing, despite the fact that it is highly important to occupational psychology in general and can certainly affect the morale and production of any workforce.

*The maintenance of interest.* If interest is conceptualised as working voluntarily at a task and expending time and effort on it, the question has to be asked concerning the maintenance of this behaviour. This is a question to which experimental psychology, at least of the behavioural kind, has a confident answer (Skinner, 1953). In general behaviour is maintained by reinforcement. The meaning of reinforcement often confuses non–psychologists because it is defined as anything which increases the probability of a response. Thus it is a truism to say that behaviour is maintained by reinforcers because this must be so by definition. However this circularity can be broken if the reinforcers can be named.

In the case of work important reinforcers are money, success and recognition that one is doing the job well, as Herzberg (1966) has argued. Thus it is clear that to keep a workforce highly motivated and interested, the job should be organised such that success is recognised and praise given. The simple gold stars of the primary school work just as well in jobs. Employees need to feel their worth and value are recognised. This applies at all levels of jobs, not simply production line workers.

The second conclusion to be drawn from the opening discussion of the notion of interest concerns its measurement. If interests are inferred from observations of behaviour in fact the best measures of interests should be based on these observations.

One approach to the measurement of interests, that of Cattell and his colleagues, has utilised this method. As was done in the fields of ability and temperament, observations of behaviour which was considered relevant to motivation were subjected to factor analysis so that the underlying factors (which would, of course, include interests) could emerge. Two tests have been developed from these studies and these will be described later in this chapter.

It was also argued that people were well aware of their interests, and the vast majority of interest tests have relied on this simple fact. Essentially they require subjects to indicate whether they are interested in certain activities or sometimes even jobs. For purposes of discussion these will be called face-valid interest tests. Problems with face-valid interest tests are detailed below.

1   Face-valid tests are easy to fake. This point has been discussed previously and there is little more to say. Clearly in the selection situation this must be a difficulty.

2   Lack of experience. This is particularly important in the case of young applicants for jobs. The concept of interest which underlies the discussion so far in this chapter has a major difficulty in that it takes no account of potential interests. A person can only be interested in what has already been tried. Most young applicants to jobs will have had no experience of many of the activities which are mentioned in the tests. Thus they will be forced to guess and in some instances they will certainly be wrong. This renders the validity of these tests dubious, at least for selection. For vocational guidance it may not be so serious, because the responses to the test will be discussed with the guidance officer and their meaningfulness can be ascertained.

I shall briefly illustrate these two problems from a study of vocational choices that I undertook many years ago, of which a brief account can be found in Kline (1975). A large sample of young people was interviewed as part of a follow up of the validity of personality and ability tests.

To test the accuracy of their claimed interests the subjects were asked to describe exactly what they did the day before, after they had assured the interviewers that this was a typical day. Thus it was discovered that those who claimed to be avid readers had never touched a book and those who loved classical music had heard not a note. Sometimes questions were asked probing claimed interests and it was quickly established when subjects were faking. Thus it was unimpressive if subjects said their favourite music was Bach (J.S.) symphonies. Such evidence as this indicated clearly that subjects had attempted to appear more cultured than in fact they were.

The second point of ignorance also quickly made itself obvious. One subject claimed that he wanted to be a biochemist. When interviewed he could not mention a single thing that a biochemist might do nor even the subjects that would have to be studied to obtain the necessary qualifications. Another less ambitious young man said that he wanted to be a long distance truck driver because in that job he could drive around the country with his wife in the cab.

These examples are not intended to prove that subjects fake their responses or respond to items about which they have no knowledge. They are included to illustrate these obvious problems with face-valid interest tests.

## Types of Interest and Motivation Test

The study of motivation has been of interest to many psychologists but relatively few tests of motivation (which is a broader term than interests) have been developed. One of the few to do so is Cattell. He has produced through factor analysis of the motivational field two tests—the Motivational Analysis Test (MAT) (Cattell et al, 1970) and the Vocational Interest Measure (VIM) (Sweney and Cattell, 1980). The MAT measures ten motivational factors, claimed to be the most important drives underlying human behaviour. However, this test is too general to appeal to personnel selectors and the VIM was developed for this more practical purpose. It remains one of the few interest tests developed through a factor analysis of the field (see Chapter 5 for a discussion of factor analysis) and this will be described later in this chapter.

One other test of interests has some sort of theoretical basis—the Vocational Preference Inventory (VPI) (Holland, 1985a). This is rooted in Holland's vocational theory which has been most recently described in Holland (1985b). The essence of this lies in the argument that there are six basic personality types and also (fortunately) six corresponding environments. People seek out the work environment which suits them best and all behaviour can be explained by the interaction between personality and environment. The VPI, as might be expected, assesses into what type each individual may be classified, thus implying what jobs would be suitable. The VPI will be described below.

The vast majority of interest tests have been developed with job selection in mind. The best known of these measures is the Strong Vocational Interest Blank and its modern incarnation, the Strong-Campbell Interest Inventory, which are described later in this chapter. These tests are completely atheoretical, the items in any scale being selected if they would discriminate one occupational group from the others. This method of test construction is known as criterion keying. A few examples will clarify the point. If the item "I enjoy working carefully with columns of figures" discriminates accountants from other occupational groups it would be used as one item in the accountancy interest scale. Similarly if the item "I enjoy being out in the fresh air regardless of the weather" discriminated forestry workers this item would go into the relevant scale. Superficially there would appear to be nothing wrong with this method of test construction but, unfortunately, there are some severe problems, which are highly relevant to personnel selection and these are discussed below.

1   Establishing adequate criterion groups. Unless the groups are very large or the occupations are highly homogeneous the criterion groups may not be representative. This means that the items which were successful in the test construction will not be as discriminating in use.

2   Differences in jobs with the same title. This can make the use of criterion keyed tests highly dubious. The most obvious example concerns lawyers. Tests developed in the USA, for example, are clearly not applicable in this country, because the job is so different. In this instance most people would not be so foolish as to attempt to use American lawyers' norms because the jobs are known to be different. But in other cases the differences may be considerable, although more subtle. A sales position is a good example where the different ethos of the jobs in the two countries is bound to affect the results.

3   Job changes. If a criterion keyed test is developed to discriminate a particular occupation, and the demands of that occupation alter, the test will cease to be useful. The most obvious example is the introduction of computers into a variety of jobs. This has rendered older criterion keyed personnel tests out of date.

4   Lack of psychological meaning of criterion keyed tests. As was discussed above these tests are empirical and atheoretical: an item is selected if it can discriminate a group. Now in the examples previously quoted the items made reasonable sense, but often in criterion keyed scales there is no obvious reason why the item discriminates and the scales are usually a complex mixture of items. This is because, of course, the occupants of different jobs differ on a variety of variables. This means that to criterion keyed scales it is not possible to attach psychological meaning. All that can be said is that they do discriminate.

This is important to personnel selection because it means that as test results are built up over the years in a variety of organisations, there is no accretion of psychological knowledge about occupational selection and success. This means that as new jobs are created and jobs change personnel managers cannot draw on psychological knowledge to decide on the test to be used in selection but have to go through a long, tedious and costly process of empirical discriminations to discover the salient variables.

For all these reasons, therefore, the use of criterion keyed tests in occupational testing should be avoided where possible. Note, however, the qualification. If other equally discriminating tests are available, preferably factored tests, these are to be preferred. However, where there are no such tests criterion keyed measures are better than nothing.

*Use of interest tests in selection.* In selection, as should be evident from previous chapters of this book, the value of psychometric tests lies in their scores. Interest tests should be chosen if it is clear from their manuals that they will discriminate the occupational groups at which the selection process is designed or if there are positive correlations between the scores and satisfaction or success at the job.

The use of interest tests in selection, where the results are used in a vague intuitive manner often considered alongside impressions gathered from interviews, has little to offer. Interest tests are quite elaborate, and expensive to buy, administer and score. To use their data in this way is no improvement on discussing job interest in an interview. If the correlations or discriminations are too low to allow quantitative or rigorous use (and this may often be so) then it is better not to use the test at all.

*Use of interest tests in appraisal.* In appraisal, however, there is a case for using interest tests, not quantitatively, but as a basis for discussion about career interests as a guide for development and possible change. If an interest test is to be utilised in this way, questions of reliability and validity are of little importance. What matters is that the test items comprise a stimulating basis for discussion; it is pointless to use a long or elaborate scale. One test which this author has found valuable for appraisal is the Rothwell-Miller Interest Blank which is described below in the list of interest and motivation tests.

Ipsative tests were discussed in Chapter 4 where it was pointed out that they should not be normed because essentially they produced nothing more than rankings of interests within each individual. This means that it is not sensible to compare individuals on such measures. However such tests are suitable for the purposes of appraisal where comparison with others is irrelevant. These points are made here because many interest tests are ipsative.

Some of the best known interest tests are set out below with a brief description. The most extensively used are American and this has obvious problems for use in Great Britain. British tests, on the other hand, are difficult to recommend for selection because they are largely atheoretical and ipsative which means that essentially they are suited only for appraisal.

Consequently in listing interest tests the most well known have been chosen which also includes those which go furthest to meet the criteria of validity, reliability and adequate standardisation, where this is appropriate. This list is not intended to be definitive since it is impossible to anticipate the needs of users. It is to be hoped that readers, on the basis of this text, will be able to select tests suited to their own purposes.

1. The Vocational Interest Measure (VIM) (Sweney and Cattell, 1980). This is one of the few objective tests, described in Chapter 5, that could conceivably be used in personnel selection. Developed by factor analysis, in an attempt to measure the most important variables relevant to interest, it contains the following scales:

1   protectiveness
2   rest-seeking
3   career
4   mechanical interests
5   clerical interests
6   scientific interests
7   aesthetic-dramatic interests
8   business interests
9   sports interests
10  nature–outdoor interests

Scale format. Although the VIM is an objective test it is in questionnaire form so that it can be given to groups.

Value in personnel work. This test is mentioned because it has been developed on a rationale which is not simply empirical. However, as yet there is insufficient evidence to justify its use other than experimentally. For example, it might be useful to administer this test to applicants and simply store the results, following up a few years later to see whether it could predict successful workers or show differences between different types of occupation.

2. The Strong Vocational Interest Blank, SVIB (Strong et al, 1971) and the Strong-Campbell Interest Inventory, SCII (Strong and Campbell, 1974). The original SVIB was produced in 1927 and it has been regularly updated since that first edition. However more recently it has been extensively revised to produce what is virtually a new test, although the test manual claims that the two are highly similar.

The original test is the most widely used interest test in the world despite all the disadvantages of its criterion-keyed method of test construction. However the SCII is the more useful test for practical selection and I shall describe only this version.

Variables.

(a) Occupational interests. Scores are compared with the scores of 57 female and 67 male occupational groups.

(b) Six general occupational scales derived from the work of Holland (whose own test is discussed below): realistic, investigative, artistic, social, enterprising, conventional.

(c) 23 basic interest scales derived from correlated items. These include: adventure, military, social services, teaching and office practice, to give a flavour of the typical occupational interests measured in this section of the test.

There are 325 items comprising activities, amusements and school subjects to which subjects have to indicate like, indifference or dislike.

Test completion time. 45–60 minutes.

The 124 occupational scales are based on American occupations and thus may not be applicable in Great Britain. There is no need to reiterate the difficulties over psychological meaningfulness which have been discussed. The six general scales and the 23 basic scales may well be more useful but these share common items and this makes their validity, other than as purely empirical discriminators, difficult to demonstrate.

Since generally the ability of interest scales to correlate with job satisfaction or success is not high, it is difficult to recommend the Strong tests, since they are so long and complex, for anything other than experimental investigation of their utility.

3. The Kuder Tests. Kuder has constructed several interest tests, which in America are the main rivals of the SVIB. The two most recent are:

(a) The Kuder General Interests Survey, KGIS (Kuder, 1970a). This measures 10 interest areas—outdoor, mechanical, computational, scientific, persuasive, artistic, literary, musical, social services and clerical.

Items. 168 of a form such that subjects have to indicate the most liked and most disliked from a triad of activities.

(b) The Kuder Occupational Interest Survey, KOIS (Kuder, 1970b). This contains 77 male occupational scales, 57 female scales and a number of academic interest scales.

Items. 100 of a form similar to the KGIS.

Comments. Both tests are ipsative and the problems of ipsative scoring have been discussed. Norms are provided but these are meaningless and can be entirely misleading. Essentially these tests are suited only for discussion with individual subjects not for comparison with others. This is particularly true of the KGIS.

The KOIS is not as disadvantaged by its ipsative scoring because items were chosen for the occupational scales if they were endorsed by members of an occupation. This means that items enter into several scales and thus subjects appear suited to a wide range of occupations. Again, as is the case with criterion keyed tests the scales are not psychologically meaningful and are dependent upon jobs not changing and being similar to the same job title in America.

Conclusions. For these reasons the scores from these tests must be treated with caution and are suited only to individual discussion. However they are far too long and complex for that purpose. Despite their considerable usage, it is difficult to recommend these Kuder tests unless they have been shown to be effective in the actual post for which selection is being made.

4. The Vocational Preference Inventory (VPI) (Holland, 1985a). This test has been developed over a number of years from Holland's extensive researches into vocational preferences. This is by far the most practicable interest inventory available for personnel selection and the only one which is likely to be useful in selection.

Variables. 11, mainly interests: realistic, investigative, artistic, social, enterprising, conventional, self-control, masculinity, status, infrequency and acquiescence.

Items. 160 occupational titles, to which subjects have to indicate like or dislike. It takes at most 30 minutes to complete.

Reliability and standardisation. The norms are derived from huge samples and reliabilities, especially of the interest scales, are beyond .8.

Comments. Holland argues that these norms are only suggestive and that local norms should be developed. The high and low scores are critical for selection and Holland has shown in more than 400 studies subjects tend to choose the occupations which suit them in terms of these interest areas.

Holland also cites correlations with various personality tests and there seems little doubt that these VPI interest scales are about the best simple indicator of interests available, although the correlations with occupational criteria are modest. It should also be pointed out that this is a good test for appraisal since it is brief, easy to administer and the items constitute a good basis of discussion.

5. Rothwell-Miller Interest Blank (Miller, 1968). This measures 12 areas of interest: mechanical, computational, outdoor, scientific, persuasive aesthetic, literary, musical, social services, clerical, practical and medical.

Items. There are 9 sets of 12 jobs. In each set the jobs have to be ranked for preference, ignoring status and money. The score is the sum of ranks.

Time to complete. 10 minutes.

Comments. This is, as the scoring makes clear, an ipsative test so that norms or comparisons of applicants' scores make no sense. This test has no external evidence for validity, since it is assumed that these job rankings reflect accurately what subjects feel. Thus psychometrically or for selection it has little to recommend it although it is probably no worse than more lengthy and elaborate tests.

However for appraisal, where the actual items can be discussed with the subjects, this is an excellent test. As a basis for discussion it is quite as good as any of the tests which have been considered and, of course, it is brief and easy to administer. Thus the Rothwell–Miller is a useful test for vocational appraisal.

It is obvious that the measurement of motivation and interest is not in an advanced state. Nevertheless the VPI is about the best supported vocational interest test, although it does little more than confirm intuitions. For appraisal and discussion the Rothwell–Miller is simple and effective. This is a field of psychometrics which merits more fundamental research perhaps along the lines of the factor-analytic Vocational Interest Measure.

# Chapter 9
# Use of Other Types of Test in Personnel Work

As might be expected, the types of test which have been discussed are not all inclusive. Psychologists have developed a variety of rather specialised tests, for example of brain dysfunction, abnormal personality and defence mechanisms, as described in psychoanalytic theory, but none of these is relevant to personnel selection or appraisal. Similarly tests of mood or emotion or tests measuring specific educational problems are not useful in personnel work.

However there are a few tests which could be of some value in selection and appraisal and these will be listed and discussed in this brief chapter.

## Tests of self-esteem

Self-esteem is a psychological variable which is widely discussed in social psychology. It would appear to be important in many spheres of activity since individuals of high self-esteem can be quietly confident and effective, with no need to put themselves forward and exhibit their brilliance, traits which are often due to low self-esteem.

Robinson et al (1991) is essentially a list and discussion of all attitude scales of any validity at all, a reference book of great value since some of these tests have not been published as tests and information about them has otherwise to be found in journals. Readers who require more information than is supplied in this chapter should consult this text.

It is clear from the work of Robinson et al (1991) that although there are huge numbers of attitude tests, the vast majority of them are not sufficiently valid or reliable to be used in personnel work except for the purposes of exploratory research.

In the case of scales of self-esteem, the present author (Kline, 1992) has concluded from a study of the validity and reliability of the best tests that despite the fact that they are reliable and correlate highly with each other there is little external support for their validity. This means that although the manuals show evidence of validity it is not to be taken at face value. In fact, the only validity these scales have is face validity.

However, if for some reason it was desirable to test self-esteem, the best test for the purposes of personnel selection is the Coopersmith Self-Esteem Inventory (Coopersmith, 1981). However the results should be treated with extreme caution and should be used only as a rough guide to self-esteem. Indeed perhaps the best use of this test is as a basis for discussion in the process of appraisal rather than as a psychometric selection test.

Items. 25 items about which subjects have to indicate "like" or "not like".

Norms. Adult norms are insufficient—a small sample of students.

Reliability and validity. Highly reliable but its validity is attested only by correlations with other self-esteem scales. Factor analyses fail to show either a general factor of self-esteem or the four aspects of self-esteem which the scale is supposed to measure.

Conclusions. A measure of self-esteem suited only for discussion in appraisal. For this purpose the best known test of self-esteem is also suitable—The Self-esteem Scale (Rosenberg, 1965) which has only 10 items.

*The Study of Values* (Allport, Vernon and Lindzey, 1960)

This is the third edition of a famous test which was first devised in 1931. Although it measures interests it is usually conceptualised as an attitude test which is why it has been discussed in this chapter rather than Chapter 8.

Variables measured. Six basic interests or motives: theoretical, economic, aesthetic, social, political and religious.

Items. The 45 items yield ipsative scores, thus making the test suited to appraisal rather than selection.

Reliability and validity. This is a highly valid test and despite the ipsative scores it will discriminate between the occupants of different jobs and students in different fields of study, and predicts value changes in individuals over almost 40 years.

Conclusions. Its ipsative scoring scheme means that this test is better suited to individual use than for comparisons, as in selection procedures. In appraisal, therefore, where results can be discussed with individuals, this is a useful test, since there is evidence that the scores do have some real psychological significance.

*The Occupational Stress Indicator, the OSI* (Cooper et al, 1988)

Variables measured. There are six scales in the OSI and a biographical questionnaire which will not be described.

1   Job satisfaction. This is broken down into five subscales: satisfaction with achievement; satisfaction with the job itself; satisfaction with organisational structure; satisfaction with organisational processes; satisfaction with personal relationships.

2   Mental and physical health.

3   Type A personality. Three subscales: attitude to living; style of behaviour; ambition.

4   Control. Three subscales: organisational forces; management processes; individual influence.

5   Job pressure. Six scales: factors intrinsic to the job; managerial role; relationship with other people; career and achievement; organisational structure and climate; home–work interface.

6   Coping with stress. Six subscales; social support; task strategies; logic; home and work relationship; time; involvement.

Items. 167 items—statements to be answered on 6-point scales.

Reliabilities. The reliabilities of many of these scales are far too low to be psychometrically acceptable. Only seven of the 28 scales have reliabilities beyond .7.

Validity. No evidence for validity is cited in the manual.

Norms. Norms are presented for British workers but the sample sizes are not given.

Comments and conclusions. At first sight this test, which was designed by some of the leading experts in this country in occupational stress, seems ideally suited to personnel work. However there are certain reservations about this test which must be discussed.

First the variables. It makes sense to divide up various aspects of job stress as the authors of the OSI have done. However, although factor analysis was used to define the variables in the construction of the test, scale 5 was constructed entirely on intuitive principles. The items were subjected to neither factor nor item analysis. This is highly unusual and is unlikely to lead to high validity. Some of the variables may require further explanation. Thus, for example, "type A personality" is a syndrome of personality traits which have been shown to be linked to the onset of heart disease. The relevance of this for personnel selection and appraisal is not easy to gauge, although, of course, it is useful if a person is showing signs of stress.

There is a further difficulty in that some of these scales have far too few items to be reliable. As was argued in Chapter 2, reliability and validity both depend upon test length, and one of the OSI scales has only three items. This accounts, to some extent, for the low reliability of many of the scales. It is worrying also that there is no attempt to demonstrate the validity of the test in the test manual.

The OSI could be a highly useful test in occupational work of all kinds. However it needs far more development. Validity studies are needed, as are more extensive norms, and more items should be written for many of the scales. However, this is a new test and it is to be hoped that over the next few years the relevant data will be collected and more items written.

# Job analysis

The whole basis for the use of psychological tests in this book has turned on fitting the right person to the right job. All the tests which have so far been discussed have been concerned with assessing the person. To conclude this chapter a test to describe jobs will be scrutinised.

The Position Analysis Questionnaire, PAQ (McCormick et al, 1972). This test was mentioned briefly in Chapter 4 and will be described here.

Variables measured. 12 factors: engaging in physical activity; operating machines; contact with the public; being aware of the work environment; performing service activities; performing clerical activities; performing technical activities; performing routine activities; supervising other personnel; working regular day schedules; working in harsh environments; having responsibilities.

Items. 194 statements relevant to some aspects of jobs which are rated on the most suitable scale, eg importance to the job or possibility of occurrence.

Discussion and conclusions. The end result of the application of the PAQ to a job is a set of ratings along the 12 factored dimensions which were set out above. From this it should be possible to estimate the psychological demands of the job and thus pick the appropriate set of tests.

However as has been argued (Kline, 1992) the PAQ cannot differentiate the level of activity involved in the job. Thus there are considerable differences between running computer programs, modifying them and inventing completely novel programs. Furthermore, despite the fact that the items in this test are general in nature, some jobs are not well described by the PAQ. In an attempt to remedy this defect, there is a special version for professional and managerial positions, the PMPQ (Mitchell et al, 1986).

Final conclusions. None of the psychological tests discussed in this chapter can be recommended unequivocally, although, as further data are collected, they may turn out to be valuable. At present they must be used with caution and are suited only to appraisal. The PAQ and the PMPQ are probably useful where a good job description is required although their utility in the selection of the right tests still remains to be proven.

# Chapter 10

# Use of Computerised Tests in Personnel Work

Just as computers have entered many jobs and occupations and changed working practices so too they have penetrated the world of psychometrics. They have done this in three ways. First they have allowed enormously sophisticated statistical analyses of test results which has led to the production of better tests. Their second impact concerns the presentation and scoring of tests and this is what will be discussed in this chapter. The third way in which computers have had their effect on psychometrics is far more fundamental. Certain tests have been developed which are entirely computer-dependent. They rely on the capability of the computer to time responses and store data. As yet these techniques are not sufficiently developed to be useful for personnel selection and appraisal, except in certain highly specialised jobs. However, the principles will be discussed because these methods will almost certainly become available for personnel work in the very near future.

It is possible to present most pencil and paper tests on the computer screen to which subjects respond by pressing a modified computer keyboard to indicate their response to each item. Most programs enable subjects to go back and alter responses if they wish.

## Advantages of Computer Presentation of Tests

(a)  The presentation is the same for all subjects. This removes any distortions caused by different explanations of the instructions.

(b)  Scoring the test can be immediate. Almost the instant the test is completed the computer can print out the results. This not only removes the tedium of scoring the test but, even more important (especially in appraisal) it allows instant feedback and discussion of results.

(c) Computer interpretation of scoring. It is possible for the computer to print out interpretations of the scores based on the norms to the test which can be stored in the computer. However, as is discussed below, these norms may not be appropriate. This is highly useful as feedback for subjects in a selection process although care has to be taken in how possibly "bad" scores are printed out. For example a low score on an intelligence test should not be printed out as "this subject is of low intelligence". Interpretations should be cautious and should be gone through with each subject by the tester to remove misunderstandings and fears about the results. To hand out computer interpretations of test scores without discussion is certainly poor practice and may be harmful for anxious individuals.

Of course such computer interpretations can be no better than the norms on which they are based. All the reservations about suitable standardisation samples, which were fully discussed in Chapter 3, apply to computer presented tests.

(d) The computer presentation of tests automatically results in the storage of the data of all subjects who take the test. This means that over a period of years without extra effort from the personnel department scores on all tests are recorded from all subjects in the organisation. This is useful for examining the validity of the tests in the selection process. For example correlations could be computed between the scores of subjects on a battery of computer presented tests and a variety of criteria 10 years after entry.

This allows the data from tests to be pooled with that from other test users, thus building up an effective compendium or library of occupationally relevant test results, across the country or even across Europe. This can be done with conventional pencil and paper tests but extra time and effort are required to insert the data into the computer.

(e) Data are recorded automatically item by item for computer presented tests. This means that statistical psychometric examination of the efficacy of the tests is possible, if desired.

Summary of advantages. The main advantage of computer presented tests compared with conventional testing procedures lies in the immediacy of the results and interpretations and the removal of the need to score the test. All this allows quick feedback to the subjects and is excellent for appraisal and career counselling and guidance.

# Problems in Computer Testing

Although the advantages of computer testing for personnel work, especially appraisal, where the rapid delivery of results is important, are obvious from the first section of this chapter, certain problems and difficulties must not be ignored.

(a) It is essential that the computer test instructions are clear and foolproof. There is no difficulty in making the instructions for operating the computer test so clear that no subjects make errors. However, as anyone who has attempted to read a computer manual must know, these can be obscure in the extreme. Obviously tests will be useless if subjects cannot master the computer.

Usually to make the administration as simple as possible a special keyboard is used, with keys exactly as required by the test. For example for the EPQ two keys "Yes" and "No" would be plugged in.

(b) Identity of conventional and computer presented tests. If a conventional test is rendered computer administrable, it is essential that the two versions are shown to be highly similar if not identical. The two versions should correlate as highly as the reliability of the original test, or even its square root.

Furthermore, new norms should be developed for the computer version of the test even if it has been shown that the two versions are highly correlated. Usually the two versions will not differ much, but this cannot be assumed.

Often, for financial reasons, the computer presented version of a conventional test will not have such new norms and this makes interpretations difficult. In the case of a test where there is a huge wealth of information such as the Cattell 16PF test or the EPQ this is particularly unfortunate (see Chapter 7), since their attraction for personnel work lies partly in the relevant occupational findings, which, on computer administration, are strictly no longer applicable. The sensible rule here is to be ultra-cautious in what use is made of the scores.

(c) The need for computers. For mass testing a large number of computers is required. Although most computer presented tests can be administered on micro-computers, to test 25 subjects together is going to cost, at present rates, around £25,000 and a programmer/technician is necessary to keep the system working. If relatively few candidates are being tested individual testing may present no problem.

(d) The availability of computer interpretations. Although it may appear to be an advantage that an interpretation of the test scores is printed out, as was stated above, this can lead to the bad practice of failed candidates in a selection procedure receiving such an interpretation with no further discussion. This too easily happens where numbers of candidates are large and there are too few personnel staff. Such practices where subjects feel mistreated and can become anxious and demoralised can lead to psychometric testing falling into ill repute thus leading the way into more pleasant but less valid selection techniques which, ultimately, are far worse for candidates.

Conclusions. It may be concluded that the computer presentation of conventional tests has definite advantages over conventional testing and that if the capability for rapid scoring and interpretation is not abused but all candidates are debriefed properly, it should be valuable. However, it is necessary to show that the computer administered test is valid and new norms should be developed.

# Tailored testing

Brief mention must be made of tailored testing which is a further application of computing to psychometric testing although one which, as yet, is restricted to rather specialised educational assessment procedures. However, as the computerised presentation of tests increases, tailored testing will be more simple to utilise in personnel work and within a relatively few years it will become common practice.

Definition of tailored testing. As the name suggests, tailored testing is essentially a bespoke version of an off the peg test. In a conventional ability test the items are arranged in order of difficulty and subjects complete as much of the test as they can within the allotted time. This is clearly a wasteful procedure for assessing the ability of any individual, since some items are too easy and others too difficult. All that is required to assess ability is to know the set of items which are on the threshold of a subject's ability. Then one can assume that all easier items would be correctly completed and all more difficult ones failed. This is what tailored testing does: it arrives at the threshold of ability for any individual without running through the whole set of items.

Outline of tailored testing procedures. In tailored testing the test is presented on a computer. However the first item is one of 50% difficulty level. If the subject gets it right, then an item at the 60% difficulty level is presented. If this is correct an item at the 70% level will be presented. If this is wrong another item at this level is presented. If wrong an item at the 65% level is presented and so on until the threshold at which the subject gets items correct and incorrect is reliably obtained. From this the subject's ability level is easily calculated.

A few points need to be noted about these tailored testing procedures.

(a) The levels of difficulty suggested in the example above are only illustrations of the technique. In fact, it is best to establish empirically with each particular set of items what difficulty gaps should be used. However these are details, the principles of tailored testing are as set out above.

(b) To work efficiently it is essential in tailored testing that the difficulty levels of items are accurate. This means that they should have been obtained from large and representative samples.

(c) It is also essential there is a large pool of items with a large selection of items at each level of difficulty.

*Advantages of tailored testing.* There are two clear advantages to tailored testing, compared to a computer presented conventional test, which recommend it for personnel work.

1. A good tailored test will be far quicker to administer than an equally good conventional test presented on a computer. In all applied applications of psychometrics, where costs are important, this gain in time is valuable.

2. Retesting is possible without necessarily using the same set of items. In tailored testing the computer selects at random from items at each level of difficulty. This means that even if applicants for a position had taken the test in another organisation their scores would not be affected to any significant extent.

*Problems with tailored testing:*

1. Tailored testing is really only suitable for variables where the items can be meaningfully ranked in order of difficulty. This means effectively that it is best with tests of ability and attainment. Although some claims have been made that it is efficient with tests of personality, far more research and evidence that it was effective would have to be provided before a tailored personality or interest test could be recommended.

2. Tailored testing can provide quick assessments of ability but their accuracy is crucially dependent upon the accuracy of the difficulty levels for each item. If these are incorrect because they were derived from small or unrepresentative samples scores will be misleading.

3. All tailored tests should have evidence that they are valid and reliable and correlate highly, at least .8, with their conventional counterparts. This is essential because, if the items have not been tried out, test error is bound to be considerable.

Conclusions. From these arguments it can be seen that tailored testing can be an efficient method of testing abilities and attainments provided that the items have been properly tried out. Within the next few years many ability tests should be available in conventional and tailored forms.

## Especially devised computer tests

It is obvious that it is possible to devise tests consisting of items and tasks which could never be part of a pencil and paper test. In fact a variety of such tests have been developed although, in their present state, it is unlikely that any would be useful in personnel work. However, as was the case with tailored testing, within the next few years it is likely that this position will have changed.

To conclude this chapter, therefore, I shall describe briefly some of these computer tests which have, in many instances, clear advantages over conventional measures, including tailored tests.

*Reaction time tests.* Jensen (eg 1987) has concentrated upon choice reaction time tests as objective measures of intelligence. In these a number of lights can be turned on. As one is illuminated the subject has to press the button corresponding to that light. The subject keeps his or her finger pressed on a home button so that "thinking" time (between the light going on and the hand leaving the home button) can be separated out from "movement" time (between the hand leaving the home button and pressing the response button).

Although there is no little dispute about the exact nature of the results and their relationship to measured intelligence (see Kline, 1991 for a discussion) there is certainly a positive correlation between intelligence and variability of reaction time and a smaller one with speed. The more complex the choice, the higher this correlation. If further research could uncover the reasons for the variability of results between investigators and precise methods of measurement, these correlations would probably rise and there would be an objective and efficient measure of intelligence.

As measures of intelligence reaction time tasks have the advantage over conventional tests in that they are hardly affected by social class or education.

*Inspection-time tests.* In this test subjects have to judge which is the shorter of two lines presented together. These lines are exposed for varying durations and the shorter the inspection time needed to make the correct decision the higher the intelligence. This is another objective measure of intelligence. Although there were early claims that this measure correlated as high as .9 with the best intelligence tests, this estimate is too high. Nevertheless, as Nettelbeck (1982) has shown, there is a substantial positive correlation, of about .5, with intelligence. Although this is not high enough for inspection time to be used as a measure of intelligence, it does mean that it might be useful in an objective computer battery of ability tests.

*Micropat* (Bartram, 1987). This is an example of a true computer test, designed for selection for pilot training. I shall describe it briefly since this will give a good indication of the kind of tests that will be useful in personnel work in the next few years.

1. There are various tracking tasks in which moving points have to be tracked on the computer screen. One has adaptive difficulty levels dependent on a subject's performance in which difficulty is varied by changing the speed or the control law. Other tasks require the coordination of hands and feet in every possible combination.

Although performance on these tasks requires similar skills to arcade video games, Bartram (1987) claims that there is no evidence that practice at such games improves test performance.

2. Tests of information management ability.

(a) Risk. One of eight keys to be used produces a penalty.
(b) Two rectangles are displayed, one smaller than the other—the signal. Then a single rectangle is presented at each trial and subjects have to decide whether this is the signal.
(c) Dual tasks. Subjects have to allocate mental resources to two tasks, a tracking task and mental arithmetic.
(d) Landing. This test resembles a simulated landing. Subjects have to allocate resources to two sources of information—visual cues on the screen and speed, fuel and height.
(e) Schedules. Five columns are displayed containing a box with a target number. To these there are five corresponding keys. If a key is pressed a line rises in the column and if it reaches the box the subject scores the number in it. However there are complicating factors: lines grow at different rates; a line and column may be erased or growth rates affected by a random variable, just for example.

Validity. This test has a correlation of .57 with pass/fail on the RAF helicopter test. This is far better than can be achieved with conventional tests.

Conclusions. Micropat is a good illustration of a battery of tests which make special use of the computer and which perform well in a specialised selection procedure. Similar tests will no doubt be developed for other similar occupations where complex information storage capacities are important. When this has been done they will be valuable in personnel selection for relevant positions. At present the province of such computer tests appears to be in the realm of abilities rather than motivation or personality. It is clear from the description of these highly effective measures that they are computer dependent, and could not be replaced by conventional tests. As has been argued, for certain positions the development of such tests will certainly aid selection and thus be valuable in personnel work.

# Chapter 11
# Interpreting Test Scores in Personnel Selection and Appraisal

It is not a difficult matter to administer a group test. Indeed anybody who can carry out instructions accurately but flexibly will be a perfectly adequate psychological tester using group tests. Similarly scoring, if not done by computer, is a matter of accuracy. As has been pointed out, most psychometric tests can be objectively scored. Interpretation, however, is not as simple. Furthermore, since the point of psychometric testing is to obtain some psychological insight into the subjects, interpretation of test scores is a critical issue.

In this chapter the various factors which have to be kept in mind in the interpretation of tests, both for selection and appraisal, will be set out and discussed. Some of the points will have been discussed before in this book but their relevance to test interpretation, which was previously implicit, will be made quite explicit.

An example of bad interpretation was briefly mentioned in the first chapter. A subject complained that he had been administered one of the Kuder tests (see Chapter 8), on which he had scored highest as a conductor of music. His careers counsellor had simply advised him to train for this occupation. This is doubly foolish, since even if the interest test had been accurate, if the subject is aged 18 without any accomplishment in music, the job would be unattainable. No enquiries on this point were made. Furthermore, it is obvious that interest in music is not sufficient to become a professional musician. Musical ability is absolutely essential. This example seems so ludicrous as to defy belief, yet, alas, it occurred and there is little doubt that similar but less glaring misinterpretations of psychometric tests are commonplace.

## Seven Guidelines for Test Interpretation

1. Psychometric test scores, even of the best tests, are not as precise or accurate as measures in the physical sciences. Thus, for example, measures of temperature

will be virtually identical, no matter what the make of thermometer. Similarly measures of time do not vary, although note that it is accepted that there may be cheap watches and clocks which are not perfectly accurate, but this is known, and allowances are made.

This is not the case in psychometrics. Even the best tests of the variable that is most accurately measured—general ability—will not give identical results. In the case of personality and motivation tests there can be considerable discrepancies.

2. Implications of test inaccuracy for interpretation. Before discussing the implications of this point readers should not feel that they have been misled into studying psychometric tests which are inaccurate. This inaccuracy is relative. Compared with interviews, or ratings based on observations over a short period of time, psychometric tests are miracles of precision. Interviews, for selection purposes, are often useless or, worse, add in error. Psychometric tests are certainly the best tools for psychological assessment and appraisal.

Set out below are the implications for personnel work of the fact that psychometric tests are imperfect measures.

(a) Small differences in scores. These should not be made too much of. For example, an IQ score of 112 is to all intents no different from a score of 113 or 114.

(b) Group scores into categories. It is sensible to divide scores into groups based upon the norms: high, above average, average, below average and low. The smallest categories should be the extremes and the largest the average category. How many subjects would fall into each of these groups depends upon the particular test and the type of candidates being tested.

Although this broad grouping overcomes many of the problems of the lack of precision of scores, it must be realised that the borderlines of the categories are thus affected. For example, if the cut-off point for the high group on a variable is 15, then a subject who scores 14 might well have been in this group on retesting. In interpreting the categories a note should be made if the subject was on a borderline.

I shall exemplify this use of categories first in selection then in appraisal and career development.

(c) Example of the use of categories in selection. Suppose that a specification equation had shown that for a particular post, say production engineer, the heaviest weightings on the 16PF test were on factors G and C, conscientious and decisive. This, of course, is a personality test (see Chapter 7) and the equation has nothing to say about abilities.

In this context, high G and C would be regarded as desirable attributes. Of the candidates judged to be satisfactory as regards engineering skills and experience, it would make sense to list those who were high on G and C. However if there was an outstanding candidate who missed the high category on G by 1 or 2 points, then it would be a misinterpretation of the tests to disregard that person on these grounds. In other words the scores have to be interpreted with some flexibility given that there is a margin of error. However a low score on these factors, if there was good evidence that they were important, should be taken fully into consideration.

(d) Example of the use of categories in appraisal and career development. Here categories should always be used, as they should when giving feedback to candidates in selection. Most people, who naturally know nothing of psychometric testing, have no grasp or intuitive insight into norms or standard scores or percentiles. However terms such as "above average" and "below average" are meaningful.

Terms such as below average and low have, for the majority of people, highly pejorative implications. Sometimes this is entirely false and sometimes these implications have some truth. It is quite hypocritical liberal egalitarianism to pretend that low intelligence, for example, indicates simply status on a variable and that there is no value judgement implied. This cannot be true since high intelligence jobs are almost always rewarded more highly than those requiring low intelligence and they almost always have more status.

Thus if any subjects are in the low category on any tests great care must be taken in explaining its meaning to them. Two examples illustrate the point—extroversion and intelligence. These have been chosen because to be low on extroversion has no pejorative meaning whereas to be low on intelligence has bad implications.

*Extroversion.* If a subject scores in the low category on extroversion, it is simple to explain that the extroversion variable is a continuum in which most people score in the middle with some high and some low scorers. The high group are typical extroverts and the low group introverts, ie quiet and restrained, bookish, preferring the company of a few close friends rather than a noisy social life, full of acquaintances. The personnel officer can easily point out that the dimension could be scored in the opposite way and introverts could be high scorers and extroverts low scorers.

There is one further point to note. In feeding back results language must be carefully chosen. Thus in the description of introverts they were described as restrained, a word with a good connotation. Although the term inhibited describes the same behaviour the connotations are quite different. It is always possible to combine accuracy without pejorative connotations. Subjects shouldnever leave a testing session, with or without feedback, feeling bad. This is a simple ethical issue.

*Intelligence.* Intelligence is certainly a different case. Again the test locates subjects on a continuum on which the majority of the population score in the middle category, with relatively few at the extremes. It is, of course, unlikely that personnel officers will get many absolutely low scorers. Their low category will be low relative to subjects who can perform the job.

Nevertheless low intelligence does have bad connotations and practical occupational implications. So to be told that one is of low intelligence cannot be explained away as simply being at the end of a continuum.

Here, therefore, the feedback must take another form. First it should be pointed out that no tests are perfect and that the score may be inaccurate in this particular case. If the subject has reasonable educational or occupational achievement this is clearly a reasonable approach, even though in this writer's experience there are indeed people with high qualifications and low intelligence. If the score is on the borderline for the group it is worth pointing this out together with the fact that on another occasion the subject could have been classified into the higher group. It can also be argued that intelligence tests test essentially abstract problem solving ability and that other abilities, for example, to sum up people accurately and to be able to get on with a variety of individuals, qualities which are sometimes referred to as social intelligence, are also important in many occupations.

Treated in this way a low score even on an intelligence test may not be regarded as an unmitigated disaster.

(e) Comparing scores on different tests. If a number of ability and personality tests have been given to a candidate it is tempting to make comparisons within the set of scores. Given the imprecision of scores it should only be done by categories, not numbers. This approach will certainly minimise test errors.

3. All standardised scores depend upon the norms. Standardised scores allow subjects to be grouped as suggested above and give meaning to the scores. However it must not be forgotten that most tests have inadequate norms, as has been discussed in Chapter 3. Corresponding to the adequacy of the norms so confidence in the meaning of the scores should vary. This means that a degree of caution about all psychometric tests should be shown. It should also be pointed out that it is essential that the norms (even if based on large samples) must be relevant to the groups being tested.

4. Where tests of rather low reliability and validity have been used (despite the warnings throughout this book) interpretations must again be cautious.

5. Do not be misled by statistics. In test manuals it is easy to find statistical studies claiming to support the utility of the test for occupational selection and appraisal, although their practical importance may be slight. For example, a test may show a statistically significant difference between engineers and therapists or a statistically significant correlation with success at a particular occupation. However, there is a big difference between statistical and psychological or practical significance and this is often forgotten by psychologists and test users.

*The meaning of statistical significance.* In statistical studies a correlation or a difference between means may be described as statistically significant. What this means is that, given the sample sizes, the correlation or mean difference of the given size could have emerged by chance (that is if there were no difference in the means and no correlation) less than 1 in 20 times (significant at the .05 level) or less than 1 in 100 times (significant at the .01 level). At these levels or beyond the results are held to be significant, not due to chance.

With this definition in mind it is easy to see that a result can be statistically significant yet of no psychological significance. Thus with 1000 subjects a correlation of .18 (say with occupational success) can be significant. However a correlation of this size (which indicates that less than 4% of variance is in common between the two sets of scores) would not make a test, on its own, useful for occupational work. Similarly with large samples a small difference in mean score, perhaps of less than two points, might be statistically significant but would not be useful in practical occupational selection.

This means that, in practice, with statistically significant findings it is necessary to look at the actual results to see whether they are of real value. If there was a large difference in scores between two groups then the findings have real application as do correlations with relevant criteria which are beyond .5.

6. Do not take the results too literally. At the beginning of this chapter was an illustration of bad test interpretation where a vocational guidance counsellor had taken a test result at its face value. Because tests are not perfect (although far superior to other methods of assessment) interpretations should be made in the context of other information.

In appraisal, especially when test scores can be discussed, the results should be interpreted as hypotheses about the individual. These hypotheses can be tested by seeing how well they fit with other information about the person—educational attainments, interests, occupational career and experience. In discussion it is possible to see whether the results seem to be supported or not.

It is possible, in appraisal, to put the findings quite directly to subjects and see whether they make sense to them although care must be taken to ensure that they do not simply agree with the test results regarding them as some kind of scientific X-ray into their character and personality.

In brief, in appraisal intelligent use of other information and sensitive discussion with subjects can maximise the efficiency of psychometric tests and render their interpretations as accurate as possible.

At this juncture one point must be stressed. This caution in interpreting the scores of tests is necessary because of their imperfect reliability and validity. If psychometric tests were more efficient it would be possible to use their scores without subjective modification. This is the aim of psychometrics and as tests improve and information concerning the relationships between success at different occupations and test scores is collected, job specifications in terms of test scores will become sufficiently accurate as to render other information of less value. However, such a prospect is in the future. For selection, especially, this is to be desired.

In selection, with the current status of testing it is best to regard the test scores as one source of information to be used alongside other data except where very high correlations between test scores and success in a particular post have already been reached. One example of this is the Micropat test, discussed in Chapter 10. Here the correlations with helicopter success are sufficiently high and other indices so unsuccessful that this test might be used unmodified, at least on an experimental basis.

7. It is essential in interpreting test scores for occupational use, especially selection but also appraisal and career development, that the tester has a thorough knowledge of the variables involved. This means far more than being simply able to describe the test variables.

There are two aspects to the psychological knowledge necessary for adequate interpretation of psychometric tests.

(a) Knowledge of the psychological nature of the variables. This can be gained from a study of the relevant psychology. This is one strong argument against having personnel testers who are trained only in testing but not in psychology. Thus to interpret scores on intelligence, extroversion and anxiety tests, for example, it is necessary to have a clear knowledge of the psychological nature of these variables and not just a vague everyday definition. For example the present author has worked with Cattell, the author of the 16PF test. As a result he has obtained a view of these variables which goes far beyond the descriptions in the Handbook. This knowledge is obtainable from a careful study of Cattell (1973) but many users of this test, in Great Britain at least, have never had the opportunity to do this.

However this defect can be overcome in a more specific way which leads to the second aspect of the required psychological knowledge.

(b) Knowledge of the test itself. Many practitioners have an adequate knowledge of the variables which they use for selection through their work and experience with the test in selection and appraisal over a number of years. For example a personnel officer may find that high scorers on I, tough-mindedness, do well in certain positions in the organisation and that in discussion, during career development, high scorers on G, conscientiousness, always do their best to discuss the implications of the test scores. This knowledge is highly valuable and stems from experience of the particular test.

This emphasis on the particular test is important because, as has been argued, two tests of what is purportedly the same variable may be far from identical. Knowledge of the test is, of course, not only derived from experience. A good test has a manual which can tell users much about the nature of the variables measured.

The other way to gain knowledge of test variables is to attend brief courses devoted to the interpretation of the tests. This is often essential where test publishers are unwilling to sell tests to individuals who have not been through their courses or have some other equivalent qualification. Except in rare instances, where the test user has an unusual knowledge of psychology and psychometrics, attendance on these courses is a highly useful way in to the necessary knowledge. Nevertheless this writer would still prefer that all test users had a good grounding, first, in psychometrics and human psychology.

Conclusions. I think it is clear from this chapter that, until tests reach a higher standard of reliability and validity and until there is a far more extensive basis of information concerning the relationship of test variables and occupational criteria, test scores will have to be modified in the light of other information and the testers' judgements. This is not to say that psychometric test scores are useless. Indeed they are by far the best source of information into the psychological characteristics of job applicants and employees involved in appraisal and career development. However, because tests are not perfectly precise, their results must be interpreted with caution and hypotheses must be tested against other information. In discussing the results of tests every effort must be made to ensure that those tested understand the implications of the results and are not made anxious or unhappy through failing to understand the meaning of the test scores.

# Chapter 12
# Developing a Selection and Appraisal System

In this chapter I shall discuss how an efficient system of selection and appraisal for all levels of personnel might be developed in the light of all that has been written in this book concerning the use and value of psychometric tests.

What are the characteristics of a good system of selection? There is no mystery or magic about the characteristics of a good selection system and these can be simply set out under a number of points.

1. The selection procedures should be cost effective. A selection system which always picked the best candidates but was extremely expensive to use would be useless unless it could be shown that such accurate selection saved the organisation money. In many cases this may not be so. If, for example, there are many able applicants a selection system need not be so perfect provided that it can eliminate those who would not be able to do the job. On the other hand, in air-crew selection, even a slight advantage in accident prevention when planes cost many millions of pounds and pilots are expensive to train, will be worthwhile.

Thus cost effectiveness depends upon the pool of applicants available and the costs of correct and incorrect selection. To estimate the cost-effectiveness of selection procedures, where the value added by every employee has to be calculated and set against his or her expenditures, is a complex matter beyond the scope of a book on psychometric testing although it should be considered in the establishment of any testing procedures. Boudreau (1989) indicates some of the problems and difficulties involved in such work. This matter will be discussed later in this chapter when assessment centres are examined.

Nevertheless, until the cost effectiveness of selection procedures has been computed, the working principle or assumption that more efficient selection benefits both employees and their organisation can be accepted unless these procedures become exceedingly expensive.

2. The selection procedures should be fair. Fairness is simply part of the ethical

procedures which have been agreed upon by working psychologists, wherever tests are used. The ethics of testing, as decreed for Great Britain, are set out and described by the British Psychological Society. There is little remarkable about them.

In essence fairness in testing means that there should be no built-in bias against particular groups, for example women or Asians. It should be noted, however, that the fact that a particular group scores low on a test is not *per se* evidence of test bias, as Jensen (1980) has argued, although such results are often used as evidence of bias.

This problem of fairness and bias is not simple. For example, it might be argued that a sound knowledge of Classical Greek was a requisite for a particular job. Such a demand, today, would effectively ensure that the job became the province of public school educated candidates. Is this demand, if there were correlations between Greek and job performance, and captains of industry still claim that there is, bias against state school educated candidates? It would be bias if it could be shown that similar predictions could be made from variables in which all candidates had an opportunity to excel. Since g, general ability, probably accounts for much of the correlation, to demand a knowledge of Greek is probably a form of bias.

3. Procedures should be seen to be fair. This, again, is all part of the ethics of testing. In the case of selection for promotion within organisations, selection which appears to be unfair leads to poor morale and work performance.

4. Selection procedures should be as valid as possible. In a sense this is an aspect of fairness since invalid procedures are by definition unfair. However, what is meant here is that all procedures should be investigated, as far as is possible, for validity and, as new ones are tried out, they can be gradually improved.

It should be remembered that with the present state of tests and other instruments of assessment, validity coefficients may not be high but, as has been previously argued, compared with interviews which are generally of zero validity, any positive correlations with criteria are improvements. All such improvements make assessment procedures more fair.

5. Selection procedures should allow a measure of feedback for all candidates. As Herriot (1989) has well argued, and this is another aspect of ethical testing, candidates should receive some feedback concerning their test performance.

6. Applicability at all levels of personnel. It is useful and probably more efficient, if the selection and appraisal system is applicable to all levels of personnel not simply the youngest and most junior. Generally selection systems follow the medical model. Here the examination system is rigorous until qualification. Then as the doctor proceeds up the career ladder, selection becomes more and more mysterious, even though there is a rough filter of College Fellowship examinations.

Choice consultantships appear to depend upon word of mouth and this, in Great Britain at least, is the sure way to inefficiency via networks of privilege and nepotism. Appointments in the higher echelons of the civil service appear to follow the same backward looking path after an initially rigorous examination, even if biased towards a public school Oxbridge group.

Conclusions. As is obvious there is little to be said concerning these desirable characteristics of selection procedures. It is clear that any methods which were cost-effective, fair, seen to be fair, valid, which allowed candidates feedback and were applicable at all levels of the organisation, would be good. These, then, are objectives. How they can be realised will be discussed below. Before this is done, however, I shall briefly discuss any further or different characteristics required of assessment for appraisal or career development.

7. Discussion and feedback essential for appraisal. As has been made clear throughout this book, tests used for appraisal have no need to be different from those used in selection since in both cases the aim is the same—to obtain a delineation of the psychological traits (ability, personality, motivation and interest) of the individuals. However the use of the results is sufficiently different to allow, in the case of appraisal, tests of lower validity than in the selection process. This is because in appraisal the results can be discussed in detail with the subjects and in some cases, for example, ipsative tests or tests with low or unknown validity are valuable since individual items can form the basis of discussion.

# Meeting the Specification of a Good System of Appraisal and Selection

Although it is easy to set out an ideal system of selection and appraisal, to establish it is a far different matter. The remainder of this chapter will be concerned with how a system which approaches this ideal as far as is possible may be established. In fact, in recent years, in Great Britain, at least, assessment centres have sprung into prominence in personnel selection and appraisal and I shall briefly describe them and discuss their value, as these represent an important attempt to set up an efficient system of appraisal and selection.

## Assessment centres

First, as Feltham (1989), who has carried out extensive research into the validity of assessment centres, argues, the term has nothing to do with any set of rooms, laboratories, or houses (the country house, for example, used for civil service selection). It refers to a selection process in which a team of judges assesses one or more candidates using a a comprehensive variety of techniques, of which one should always be a work sample or a simulation, ie an exercise in which elements of the job have to be executed. Other techniques include interviews and psychometric tests of ability, personality and interests.

From the assessment centre emerges a report which combines qualitative and quantitative information. The qualitative consists of accounts of the candidates' strengths and weaknesses, the quantitative of the test scores and ratings, all concluding in decisions to select, to promote or not as the case may be, and, in respect of appraisal, recommendations involving feedback, career planning and future training. Assessment centres are used most frequently by organisations to assess management potential but there is no reason why they cannot be used for personnel selection and appraisal at any level.

From this description by Feltham (1989) it is clear that assessment centres are one particular method of putting into practice the recommendations concerning the proper interpretation of psychometric tests, set out in the final paragraph of Chapter 11. It was argued there that, because of the defects of these tests, it was necessary to combine their results with other information. This is precisely what assessment centres do. Thus the discussion of assessment centres must now turn to the question of whether assessment centres are the best method of integrating other information and whether this other information is what should be integrated. This is particularly important because there can be no doubt that some other input, say from projective tests such as the Rorschach, would worsen rather than improve the processes of selection and appraisal. To answer these questions a few further points need to be made.

*Costs of assessment centres.* As Feltham (1989) points out, assessment centres are expensive: costs include job analysis, purchase and development of tests and exercises, training assessors, hiring accommodation, travel and staff time. Centres last from one to three days and if internal staff are being assessed there may be further time to be spent on feedback.

*The validity of assessment centres.* Since assessment centres use many different techniques care has to be taken in assessing studies of their validity. Thus if a centre is shown to be valid it does not demonstrate that any other centre would be so with different tests, other different methods of assessment, different staff and different jobs.

Feltham (1989), in his excellent summary paper, concludes from an examination of the studies of validity that if assessment centres are well designed they seem to be effective but if they are quickly designed, with little professional input, they are likely to be worthless. However this is only useful advice if the meaning of well designed can be clarified. In fact this means good job analysis (see Chapter

4), good simulations and exercises and these are dependent on good job analysis, good psychometric tests and careful training of assessors.

However, even the best results with assessment centres are far from perfect. Thus studies of their validity for the administrative civil service, in a 30-year follow-up, showed that 40% of those rated best reached the topmost rank, while of those who just passed only 12% reached these grades. This undoubtedly supports the validity of assessment centres but there was still considerable error. Put another way 60% of those rated best did not reach the top grades.

*Problems with assessment centres.* Reliability. The reliability of judgements concerning performance between assessors, even when they are well trained, is lower than is desirable. Furthermore, as Feltham points out, many of the ratings made of performance are not independent. In addition it has been shown that the discussions among raters of their scorings before the final judgement of candidates adds nothing to validity or reliability. In other words the additional information from the work simulation may be valuable but all depends upon the accuracy of the simulation and the skill of the raters. As was mentioned above, cheap and quick assessment centres are virtually useless.

Simulation exercises. The validity of these exercises depends upon adequate job analyses which, as has been discussed, are no easy task. Furthermore even if they are good, rating them is fraught with error.

*Cost benefits.* As has been seen, good assessment centres are expensive to set up and run. Feltham attempts to justify this expenditure in terms of ultimate benefits. He argues that even a few thousand pounds per selected candidate may not be excessive particularly when headhunters for management positions charge about a third of the starting salary. He argues that the monetary benefits of using an assessment centre, assuming that it is of reasonable validity, are huge compared with selection by unsophisticated methods such as interviews. Since the justification for setting up any selection system must be its cost effectiveness it is necessary to examine this issue in a little more detail both in respect of assessment centres and other possible selection and appraisal systems.

Cost benefits of assessment centres and other systems of selection and appraisal. First it should be noted that the claim of Feltham (1989) that the cost benefits of selection centres are huge compared with unsophisticated methods such as interviews is not powerful from the viewpoint of psychometric testing. There can be no doubt that psychometric tests would also be highly cost effective compared with interviews. As has been stressed throughout this book, interviews are of generally low validity in selection.

What is important, therefore, in estimating the cost effectiveness of assessment centres is to know how much more effective they are than psychometric tests alone. Utility analysis, which attempts to quantify cost benefits of selection systems takes account of quantity (number of personnel and the length of time), quality (the consequences of the selection in terms of money) and the costs. Clearly there are problems in the accurate quantification of these variables although in the case of air force training, where the cost of training is known and the costs of planes are fixed, quantification is easier than in most jobs. In general the cost benefits of assessment centres appear to be positive. However, this may be attributed to the psychometric procedures rather than the exercises and interviews of the assessment centre.

However, in Chapter 11 it was pointed out that although psychometric tests of the kinds recommended in the earlier chapters of this book are the most valid assessment measures which have so far been devised, it was also argued there that they were not so efficient that the results should not be tempered by other methods. Indeed only in the case of intelligence tests would the present writer rely entirely on the scores, although even here it is necessary to make sure that scores have not been lowered by anxiety. Thus, the critical question becomes further refined. Psychometric test scores at present require some additional data, but are these of the kind provided by the assessment centre?

The answer to this question turns on the term assessment centre. It was pointed out at the beginning of this section that this refers to a set of procedures in which simulation or job sampling plays a part. Now this means that it is certain that for different jobs simulation and job sampling will not be equally efficient. For example the attempt to simulate military tasks is always rendered difficult because the effects of stress and danger cannot be included in the exercise. On the other hand job samples of civil service work (not the drinking of tea) can be devised and it is noteworthy that it was in the civil service that assessment centres were shown to be useful. Given this problem it seems that there can be no general answer to the question. In some cases assessment centres may be efficient. However if the term is widened beyond its normal usage to include a set of assessment procedures, including psychometric tests, then it follows from all the arguments in this book that assessment centres are useful in selection.

Conclusions. From this discussion of assessment centres some clear conclusions relevant to setting up a system of personnel appraisal and selection can be drawn. I shall set them out under a number of headings.

1   Psychometric testing should form the backbone of any appraisal and selection system. Psychometric tests, properly constructed and validated, are the most valid instruments of psychological assessment.
2   Even the best psychometric tests are of imperfect validity and their scores need to be tempered with other information.
3   Assessment centres are one form of obtaining other useful information.

4   In their traditional form with work samples or simulations it is difficult to justify their use for all selection posts.

5   Well trained interviewers with properly planned interviews designed sensibly to amplify psychometric test scores are probably sufficient to maximise the value of psychometric tests.

6   Other methods, such as simulations or job samples, should be used only where there is clear evidence that they are adding to the validity of the selection procedures beyond the psychometric tests. This leads on to the final point.

7   All selection methods and appraisal methods should be validated. To conclude this chapter, therefore, the role of the evaluation of selection and appraisal procedures in personnel work is discussed briefly.

*Need for evaluation.* In personnel work it is important to investigate the validity of all procedures simply because none is perfect and there should be constant experiment and attempts at improvement, all of which need validation.

*Difficulties in evaluation.* There are considerable difficulties in evaluating selection procedures, the main one being the impossibility of following up those who are not selected. However in a large organisation it is possible to monitor the progress of those selected for various positions and relate this to their assessments.

Where a large number of applicants has been taken on these can be grouped into pass, above average and superior and the progress of the groups can be compared. This is a far from ideal approach, however, because in some cases promotion may be partly influenced by outstanding performance in the entry procedures. Nevertheless if the lowest group were doing just as well as the other groups, or better, something is wrong with the selection.

If there is general satisfaction with recruits in the organisation and with workers who have been promoted after assessment, this is clearly not bad evidence for the efficacy of the selection and appraisal system. However it cannot be regarded as strong support because there is no way of knowing how those not selected would have fared. All that can really be said is that it is better than dissatisfaction with the quality of the personnel or where it is clear from the performance of the individuals that they are incapable of filling the post.

Ideally, in any assessment procedure the efficacy of the parts as well as the whole should be evaluated. This is particularly important, as has been argued, in the study of assessment centres where it is essential to know how much validity has been increased over and above that of the psychometric tests. Such an analytic procedure also permits the evaluation of any new, experimental tests or other forms of assessment.

Perhaps the most effective evidence for the validity of a selection and appraisal system might spring from a demonstration of its cost effectiveness. Certainly if the cost utility of the system were demonstrated it could not be said to be worthless. However it should be noted that even where the cost benefits of a system have been demonstrated, this does not mean the selection system is valid. It might have selected efficient individuals but not the most efficient, ie some of the rejects might still have been better than some of those accepted. Despite this caveat, the demonstration of cost benefits is valuable.

From this it is clear that evaluation is a necessary part of any selection or appraisal system especially where the system is not perfectly precise.

Final conclusions. The results of this discussion are clear: any adequate system of selection and appraisal should have as its basis the best psychometric tests of ability, personality and interest, as described in earlier chapters of this book. These tests need to be supplemented by other information which, in most cases, is best obtained by carefully planned interviews by trained interviewers. There is, at present, no justification for more elaborate assessment centres for every selection procedure, although with careful research job samples and simulations could be made useful. Cost benefit analyses are the best support for selection systems and ultimately these should be undertaken. This forms part of the evaluation procedures which should be a central aspect of any system of selection and appraisal.

# Chapter 13
# Conclusions and Summary

In this chapter will be found a concise summary of the main points and conclusions concerning psychometric testing in personnel selection and appraisal. Each point is succinct and numbered. The rationale and arguments in support of them will be found in the relevant chapters.

1    Definition of a psychometric test: a psychological test, usually consisting of a set of items and with norms for comparing scores. They are almost always objectively scored.

2    The psychometric model. This is a model of human behaviour which claims that all behaviour is explicable in terms of factors of ability, personality, motivation and state or mood together with the situation in which individuals find themselves. This is the model underlying the use of tests in personnel work.

3    Good psychometric tests possess certain valuable characteristics:
    (a) they are reliable, meaning that they are consistent and that they are stable over time. A minimum reliability is .7, essential for reducing the standard errors of scores
    (b) they are valid, meaning that they measure what they claim to measure. There are various forms of validity: concurrent validity, predictive validity, and construct validity. Face validity refers to the appearance of validity, from the viewpoint of the subject
    (c) they are discriminating, thus producing a good spread of scores
    (d) they have good norms, the scores of well defined groups on the test. Norms should be based on large and representative samples.

4    Ipsative tests. Some psychometric tests are ipsative, that is their scores are derived from forced choice items. These scores cannot yield meaningful norms and individuals should not be compared on ipsative scores. They are suited only to individual discussion.

5 Tests used in personnel selection and appraisal must be highly reliable, valid, possess good norms (information to be found in the test manual) and be brief and simple to administer.

6 There are various methods of deciding what variables to measure in selection and appraisal:

(a) select the main variables in the fields of ability, personality and interests or motivation

Abilities: fluid and crystallised intelligence; retrieval; visualisation; cognitive speed

Personality: extroversion; anxiety or neuroticism; conventionality; conservatism and tough-mindedness

Motivation and interest: no agreement concerning the main variables

(b) discover the important variables through task or job analysis

(c) choose variables which correlate with success at the job

(d) choose variables which discriminate the relevant occupational group from other groups.

7 Psychological tests fall into several clear categories:

(a) ability tests. These include intelligence tests, measuring g, general ability, verbal, numerical and spatial ability together with specific ability tests

(b) aptitude tests. Some aptitude tests are simply measures of ability, eg verbal aptitude. Others are mixtures of variables such as clerical or programming aptitude

(c) personality tests fall into three types: personality questionnaires, projective methods and objective tests. Only the first is suited to personnel selection and appraisal

(d) motivational tests which include tests of state or mood, such as anxiety, and interest tests

(e) other types. These include special clinical and neuropsychological tests which would not be used in personnel work.

8 Intelligence tests are almost always useful in personnel work while other ability tests are useful in certain cases although often qualifications may be a sufficient guide to special abilities.

9 Useful intelligence and ability tests in personnel work are: Raven's Matrices, Mill-Hill Vocabulary Scale, Watson-Glaser test, the AH series of tests, the Comprehensive Ability Battery by Cattell.

10 Personality inventories are valuable in personnel work both for selection and appraisal, although there are problems with faking and response sets.

11   Useful personality tests in personnel work are: the EPQ, and Cattell's 16PF test.

12   The measurement of interests is not as well developed as that of personality and ability. Many tests are ipsative and thus suited only to discussion in appraisal and many are American and thus not necessarily suited to use in Great Britain.

13   Nevertheless a few interest tests may be useful in selection and appraisal in some cases. These are: the VIM, the Strong-Campbell Interest Inventory, the Kuder Tests and the Vocational Preference Inventory. For appraisal the brief Rothwell–Miller is useful.

14   Other types of test. Certain tests which do not fit into the main categories could be useful in personnel work. These include: the Coopersmith Self-esteem Inventory, the Study of Values, the Occupational Stress Indicator, and for job analysis the Position Analysis Questionnaire.

15   For personnel work computer-presented tests have definite advantages over conventional tests—especially the immediacy of scoring, and the printout of results for discussion and feedback. Automatic storage of results is also useful for the development of data bases and in-house norms. However for group testing a large number of computers is needed.

16   A computer-presented test must be shown to be equivalent to the original, conventional form.

17   Tailored testing where the items, presented by computer, are chosen specifically for each individual can be useful in personnel work for such tests are brief and efficient. However tailored tests are suited only to tests of ability and attainment, especially the latter.

18   Certain psychological tests depend entirely on the computer. For certain specific occupations these may be the best form of test. One example is the Micropat battery for helicopter pilot selection.

19   Test interpretation in personnel work requires a sound knowledge of the tests and preferably the underlying psychology.

20   Test scores are not so precise that they should be used literally. It is best to categorise scores, eg into high, low and average, and to interpret them in the light of other information about the subjects.

21   Statistical significance should not be confused with psychological significance.

22   Assessment centres, which use a variety of assessment methods including work samples are useful in some selection and appraisal situations. However they are expensive and poorly conducted assessment centres are useless.

23    Assessment centres should be evaluated with reference to the particular occupation involved. It is important to see what extra validity is added by the centre beyond the psychometric tests.

24    A good selection and appraisal system will be based on psychometric tests but will use other additional data not necessarily as elaborate as that of an assessment centre.

25    The validity of all selection and appraisal systems should be evaluated every few years so that improvements can be made.

26    Ideally the cost benefits of the selection system should also be worked out.

27    In conclusion, the efficiency of a selection and appraisal system depends ultimately on the efficiency of its psychometric tests. As these are improved and developed the need for other methods of appraisal will disappear.

# References

Allport, G W, Vernon, P E & Lindzey, G, *Study of Values: Manual and Test Booklet*. Houghton Mifflin, 1960

Anastasi, A, *Psychological Testing*. Macmillan, 4th edition, 1976

Bartram, D, "The development of an automated testing system for pilot selection: the Micropat system" in *Applied Psychology: An International Review* 36. 1987

Boudreau, J W, "Selection utility analysis: a review and agenda for future research" in M Smith & I T Robertson (eds), *Advances in Selection and Assessment*. Wiley, 1989

Briggs, K C & Myers, I B, *The Myers-Briggs Type Indicator*. Educational Testing Service, 1962

Buros, O K (ed), *The Fifth Mental Measurement Yearbook*. Gryphon Press, 1959

Buros, O K (ed), *The Seventh Mental Measurement Yearbook*. Gryphon Press, 1972

Cattell, R B, *Personality and Mood by Questionnaire*. Jossey-Bass, 1973

Cattell, R B, Eber, H W & Tatsuoka, M M, *The Sixteen Factor Personality Questionnaire*. Institute for Personality and Ability Testing, 1970

Cattell, R B, Horn, J L & Sweney, A B, *Motivation Analysis Test*. Institute for Personality and Ability Testing, 1970

Child, D, *Essentials of Factor Analysis*. Holt, Rinehart & Winston, 2nd edition, 1991

Cook, M, *Personnel Selection and Productivity*. Wiley, 1990

Cooper, C L, Sloan, S J & Williams, S, *Occupational Stress Indicator*. NFER-Nelson, 1988

Coopersmith, S, *Self-Esteem Inventory*. Consulting Psychologists Press, 1981

Costa, P T & McCrae, R R, *The NEO Personality Inventory*. Odessa, 1988

Cronbach, L J, *Essentials of Psychological Testing*. Harper & Row, 4th edition, 1984

Eysenck, H J & Eysenck, S B G, *The Eysenck Personality Questionnaire*. Hodder & Stoughton, 1975

Eysenck, H J, Eysenck, S B G & Barret, P, *The Eysenck Personality Questionnaire* (Revised). Hodder & Stoughton, 1992

Feltham, R T, "Assessment Centres" in P Herriot (ed), *Assessment and Selection in Organisations*. Wiley, 1989

Ghiselli, E E, *The Validity of Occupational Aptitude Tests*. Wiley, 1966

Hakstian, A R & Cattell, R B, *The Comprehensive Ability Battery*. Institute for Ability and Personality Testing, 1976

Heim, A W, Watts, K P & Simmonds, V, *AH4, AH5 and AH6 Tests*. NFER, 1970

Heim, A W, Watts, K P & Simmonds, V, *AH2 and AH3 Tests*. NFER, 1974

Herriot, P (ed), *Assessment and Selection in Organisations*. Wiley, 1989

Herzberg, F, *Work and the Nature of Man*. Staples Press, 1966

Holland, J P, *The Holland Vocational Preference Inventory*. Consulting Psychologists Press, 1985a

Holland, J P, *Making Career Choices: A Theory of Personality Types and Work Environments*. Prentice-Hall, 1985b

Jensen, A, *Bias In Mental Testing*. Free Press, 1980

Jensen, A, "The g beyond factor analysis" in R R Royce, J A Glover, J C Conoley & J C Witt (eds), *The Influence of Cognitive Psychology on Testing*. Erlbaum, 1987

Jewell, L N & Siegall, M, *Contemporary Industrial/Organisational Psychology*. West Publishing Co, 2nd edition, 1990

Katz, M R, "The Strong Vocational Interest Blank" in O K Buros (ed), *The Seventh Mental Measurement Yearbook*. Gryphon Press, 1972

Kline, P, *The Psychology of Vocational Guidance*. Batsford, 1975

Kline, P, *Intelligence: The Psychometric View*. Routledge, 1991

Kline, P, *A Handbook of Psychological Testing*. Routledge, 1992

Kuder, G F, *Kuder General Interest Survey*. Science Research Associates, 1970

Kuder, G F, *Kuder Occupational Interests Survey*. Science Research Associates, 1970

McCormick, E J, Jeanneret, P R & Mecham, R C, "A study of job characteristics and job dimensions as based on the Position Analysis Questionnaire (PAQ)" in *Journal of Applied Psychology* 56. 1972

Miller, K E, *The Rothwell-Miller Interest Blank*. NFER, 1968

Mitchell, J L, McCormick, J, Jeanneret, P R, McPhail, S M & Mecham, R C, *The Professional and Managerial Position Questionnaire*. Purdue Research Foundation, 1986

Nettelbeck, T, "Inspection time: an index for intelligence" in *Quarterly Journal of Experimental Psychology* 24a. 1982

Raven, J C, *Progressive Matrices*. H K Lewis, 1965

Raven, J C, *Mill-Hill Vocabulary Scale*. H K Lewis, 1965

Robinson, J P, Shaver, P R & Wrightsman, L S (eds), *Measures of Personality and Social Psychological Attitudes*. Academic Press, 1991

Rosenberg, M, *Society and the Adolescent Self-Image*. Princeton University Press, 1965

Skinner, B F, *Science and Human Behaviour*. Macmillan, 1953

Strong, E K & Campbell, D P, *Strong-Campbell Interest Inventory* (revised edition). Stanford University Press, 1974

Strong, E K, Campbell, D P, Berdie, R E & Clerk, K E, *Strong Vocational Interest Blank*. Stanford University Press, 1971

Sweney, A B, Anton, M T & Cattell, R B, *The Vocational Interest Measure*. Institute for Personality and Ability Testing, 1980

Vernon, P E & Parry, J B, *Personnel Selection in the British Forces*. University of London Press, 1949

Watson, G & Glaser, G M, *Critical Thinking Appraisal*. Harcourt Brace Jovanovich, 1964

# Appendix
# Further Reading

The books selected in this appendix for further reading fall into two categories.

1. Some are concerned with industrial or occupational psychology in general. These are valuable because selection and appraisal is affected by the type of organisation in which they take place and these contextual factors need to be understood by personnel workers. Similarly factors influencing job satisfaction should be appreciated, in addition to the techniques of testing.

2. A second category deals with psychometrics. The present book is brief in the extreme and these readings illuminate various important aspects of psychometrics, both theory and testing.

In all cases I have suggested books which are as easy to read as is possible, given the type of material with which they are concerned. Some topics such as the statistical basis of psychometrics are inevitably difficult but this is the exception.

Cattell, R B & Johnson, R C (eds), *Functional Psychological Testing*. Brunner Mazel, 1986. This is a book edited by Cattell, who is one of the leading psychologists in the world, with chapters by his colleagues. It contains an excellent account of both the theory and practice of testing with several chapters highly relevant to occupational selection and appraisal. However it should be read bearing in mind that almost all the tests and methods recommended are those of Cattell and his colleagues. Nevertheless, it should be read by all involved in personnel work.

Cook, M, *Personnel Selection and Productivity*. Wiley, 1990. This is another book which should be read by all engaged in personnel work. It is a useful complement to the present book since it deals with all other aspects of industrial psychology and the chapters on testing are extremely brief. It is particularly valuable since it is easy to read and the author is both practitioner and academic, a good combination in this field.

Herriot, P (ed), *Assessment and Selection in Organisations*. Wiley, 1989. This is a huge edited book with chapters on virtually every topic relevant to selection and appraisal and personnel work in general. This is a valuable resource book with good references to all aspects of the subject. In addition with chapters by academics and practitioners it has a wide appeal. However, as with all edited books, despite the heroic efforts of the editor, it suffers from the problem of the uneven standard of chapters which range from simplistic to highly complex. Nevertheless the majority are clear and informative: a valuable reference text.

Holland, J. P, *Making Career Choices: A Theory of Personality Types and Work Environments*. Prentice-Hall, 1985. Holland is one of the leading theorists in the field of occupational choice and has produced one of the most practical measures of interests for personnel selection, the VPI. This book should, therefore, be read by all practitioners.

Jensen, A, *Bias in Mental Testing*. Free Press, 1980. This book convincingly answers the charge that intelligence tests are inherently biased against certain groups. However it does far more than this and provides a detailed delineation of the nature of intelligence and intelligence tests.

Jewell, L N & Siegall, M, *Contemporary Industrial/Organisational Psychology*. West Publishing Company, 2nd edition, 1990. This book describes all aspects of occupational psychology, not only selection and appraisal. It is extremely useful background reading since, as was indicated, selection and appraisal take place within organisations, the nature of which is a considerable influence on them. Personnel workers should be fully aware of these factors, as well as with the general psychology of organisations.

Kline, P, *A Handbook of Test Construction*. Methuen, 1986. This is one of the few accounts of how to construct tests which includes chapters on the statistical techniques and writing items. It is designed to be a practical guide which can be followed without extensive training. It will be useful for personnel workers who want to develop their own specific in-house tests.

Kline, P, *Intelligence: The Psychometric View*. Routledge, 1991. This is a brief summary of recent work in the psychometrics of intelligence. This answers the foolish attempts (by the statistically ignorant) to deny the importance of general ability in understanding human performance. Since intelligence tests are central to personnel work, their theoretical basis should be understood.

Kline, P, *A Handbook of Psychological Testing*. Routledge, 1992. This is a comprehensive account of all aspects of psychological testing. Almost all the topics dealt with in *Psychometric Testing in Personnel Selection and Appraisal* are discussed in detail. Particularly useful will be the sections on psychometric theory, test construction, types of test and the detailed discussions of particular tests and their uses, at the end of the book.

Nunnally, O, *Psychometric Theory*. McGraw-Hill, 1978. This is by far the clearest account of the statistical basis of psychometric testing. It is not an easy book but it is comprehensible with effort. There is no doubt that an understanding of psychometric theory improves radically the evaluation, construction and application of psychometric testing.

Vernon, P E & Parry, J B, *Personnel Selection in the British Forces*. University of London Press, 1949. I make no excuse in suggesting such an old book. For nearly 50 years Vernon was one of the leading psychometrists who could also write with great clarity. The work of Vernon and colleagues in personnel selection, described in this book, is of the highest standard. If all selection were like this, there would be no need for the present book. It is a fine example of careful selection and evaluation of all procedures.

## Other sources of information about psychometric tests

The results of research with tests are reported in psychological journals. Papers submitted to the best of these journals are refereed so that in general they are technically sound. Journals where test results relevant to personnel work are published and which are readily comprehensible are set out below:

*Personality and Individual Differences*
*Journal of Occupational Psychology*
*Personnel Psychology*
*Journal of Applied Psychology*

Occasionally relevant papers appear in the more general psychological journals. References to such articles may be found in the suggested readings and in the journals above.

*Mental Measurement Yearbooks*. These appeared every five years and were edited by Oscar Buros. They contain descriptions and evaluations of all tests published in the USA and UK. These have been discussed in Chapter 4 of the present book. Recent editions have a new editor.

*Catalogues of test publishers*. These contain useful details and descriptions of tests provided that it is remembered that these are commercial organisations. The main test publishers were listed in Chapter 4 of the present book.

# Index